I AM LUBO

The incredible story of a child's struggle to survive.

LOU PECHI

*

Print Edition 2012
Revision 4

Library of Congress Card Number
LCCN 2012921092

Pechi, Lou
I am Lubo: The incredible story of a child's struggle to survive.

Summary: A true story of growing up, before, during, and after the Holocaust. It tells about a child's struggle, not only to survive, but also to keep his true identity throughout those difficult years.

ISBN 978-1-47810-896-2

Additional photographs, chronology, backup documents, original letters, and contact information can be found on the website:

www.iamlubo.com

Dedication

*To all those
who risked their lives
to save mine.*

Lou Pechi

Table of Contents

Acknowledgements

This memoir, in the making for the last thirty years, would not have happened without the encouragement and assistance of friends, acquaintances, and even strangers who, after hearing my story, insisted that I should write it.

In December of 1998 I testified for the Steven Spielberg's Survivors of the Shoah Visual History Foundation. My taped three-hour interview became the framework for my book. I am grateful to Mr. Spielberg for allowing me and thousands of Holocaust survivors to provide personal testimony of their experiences. The DVDs of our testimonies are available from USC's Shoah Foundation Institute.

I am thankful to Kathy Diamant, author of *Kafka's Last Love* and numerous travel articles, for many suggestions and her constructive advice. When I was a student in her Memoir Writing Class through San Diego State University's Osher Lifelong Learning Institute, she urged me to put all my loose material into a single manuscript and give it a working title. Classmates also provided me with helpful critiques; I am especially indebted to Alice Lowe and Jim Brega. During our weekly discussions they provided valuable suggestions for my writing.

My sincere gratitude goes to Daniele Ceschin, whose *In Fuga da Hitler* book I found in Italy. His book lists my name, and those of many Jewish refugees interned during WW II in Treviso, Italy. Mr. Ceshin discovered the police archives of that period and was kind enough to send me copies of documents related to my family.

I am grateful to Esther Gitman, author of *When Courage Prevailed* for reading my first draft and providing valuable feedback, comments and encouragement.

Anne Marie Welsh, dance critic for the San Diego Union-Tribune for the last 25 years and author of five books (Time for Kids, Scholastic) edited the final manuscript, and I am immensely grateful for her most helpful comments and constructive critique.

My greatest thanks go to Fergal O'Doherty for working with me weekly for the last year. His knowledge, insight and perceptive comments added so much to the content of *I Am Lubo*.

And I would, of course, be remiss not to mention Lenore, my dear wife, who provided meaningful suggestions and proofread much of the manuscript.

I hope this book will be a legacy to my son Tony, my daughter Nina, my grandchildren Dan, David, and Julia, and to future generations of our family.

—

Blank Page

After Charles Bukowski's poem, "Bluebird".

I have a page that's blank and white,
It's calling me to write.
Thoughts floating in my mind
Are fighting to break out.

Memories of early days,
Faded and worn out,
Flicker, hide, and reappear,
As they fight to get out.

The songs I used to sing and hear
Whimsical, light and gay
Keep humming their melodies
Dancing to get out.

I wonder if I ever can
Express what's in my heart.
I know it's I who has to fight
To free, and let them out.

Lou Pechi

Prologue

MASS ATTACK, GERMANS OVER BELGRADE, GOVERNMENT REPORTED TO HAVE WITHDRAWN

LONDON, United Kingdom

A neutral observer at Berne reported that 250 German planes participated in this morning's attack on Belgrade, and that a ten-minute air-raid alarm was sounded. . . .

Evening Post, Monday, April 7, 1941

OPERATION PUNISHMENT

The sun rose early in Belgrade on April 6 (Palm Sunday). The sky was lavender blue and clear with the promise of a crisp spring day. People were already bustling in the streets when at 5 a.m. a telephone bell alerted General Mirković at Air Command headquarters, eighty miles to the north, that an observation post at Serb reported 50 aircraft flying in tight formation from Hungary toward the capital.

Marshall Cavendish, *History Of The Second World War*

AERIAL DRIVE IS GREATEST IN ATTACKS ON YUGOSLAVIA, GREECE
BERNE, Switzerland

The death toll in Belgrade as a result of dive-bombing attacks, wrecking portions of the central part of the capital, was reported heavy, with 73 dead in the first raid . . .

The Nazi radio, in broadcast "eyewitness" accounts by German pilots, said the exposed city was "a sea of flames."

The Stukas have begun their work of destruction before us. Fires are aglow over Belgrade. Belgrade is a sea of flames. . . .

The Belgrade radio went dead during the first German aerial bombardment of the Yugoslav capital. . . .

The New York Times, Monday, April 7, 1941

THE AIR BOMBARDMENT OF BELGRADE
The Luftwaffe opened the assault on Yugoslavia by conducting a saturation-type-bombing raid on the capital Belgrade in the early morning hours of 6 April 1941. Flying in relays from airfields in Austria and Romania, 150 bombers and dive-bombers protected by a heavy fighter escort participated in the attack. The initial raid was carried out at fifteen-minute intervals in three distinct waves, each lasting for approximately twenty minutes. Thus, the city was subjected to a rain of bombs for almost one-and-a-half hours. The German bombardiers directed their main effort

against the center of the city, where the principal government buildings were located.

The weak Yugoslav Air Force and the inadequate flak defenses were quickly wiped out by the first wave, permitting the dive-bombers to come down to roof-top levels. Against the loss of but two German fighters, twenty Yugoslav planes were shot down and forty-four were destroyed on the ground. When the attack was over, more than 17,000 inhabitants lay dead under the debris.

Jason Pipes, *Luftwaffe - The Air Force 1935-1945*
http://www.feldgrau.com/yugowar.html

Life in Zagreb was peaceful until that day.

From then on, nothing would be the same.

Lou Pechi

Map of Croatia, Yugoslavia, and Italy

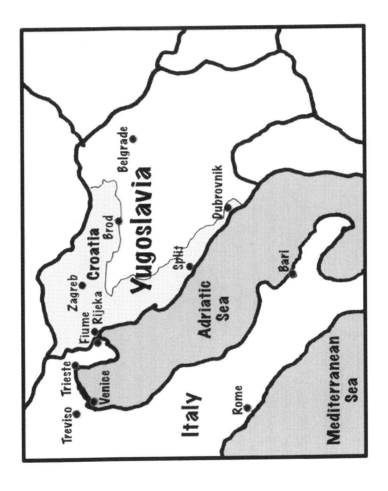

Lou Pechi

<u>BEFORE THE STORM</u>

Zagreb - Mutika, Lubo, Kolega

Zagreb "Fräulein" and Lubo

Zagreb – Lubo

Zagreb – Lubo

Juan Les Pins, France –
Lubo, Mutika, Aunt Anika, Uncle Milan

The Traffic Policeman

It's a bright June day in 1938 in Zagreb, my hometown. I am almost four. Every month father takes me to our barber downtown to get a haircut. My father is funny, kind, loving, and always helpful. He is the best friend I have. I call him, *"Kolega"*, Croatian for "Colleague."

This morning he puts on a freshly ironed white shirt. The clean scent of laundry soap wafts from the starched white cloth. Under the stiff collar, he wraps a vivid paisley patterned tie. He carefully ties the cloth into a triangular knot held by his right hand. He pulls the other end with his left, tightening the noose around his neck. I see my face reflected in the polished black shoes he slips on his feet. He straightens up and puts on his suit jacket. When I grow up, I want to be tall like him and dress in a suit and tie. I will wear shiny black shoes, and not the children's brown lace-up shoes Kolega puts on my feet. I will wear long pants, and not the short pants with suspenders I am wearing now.

Kolega helps me with my coat and we go out the front door. He reaches for his hat on the rack and puts it on. The hat makes him look taller than he really is. When I grow up I will also wear a hat like his.

We leave the house and walk downtown. I hold Kolega's hand and look proudly up to him. He is more than my father. He is my Kolega, and my best friend.

The broad boulevard is lined with linden trees speckled with yellow flowers. They fill our nostrils with a sweet honey smell. Their broad green leaves shade us from the morning sun. We approach the tall downtown buildings flanked by wide sidewalks full of people dressed in their finest clothing. Dark suited men, walk in a sea of vibrant colors of women's dresses. Bright bonnets weave among plain brown and black men's hats, like colorful fish swimming in a dark river. The morning traffic is hectic, a chorus of humming motors, auto horns, and squealing brakes. Black cars dodge blue trolleys that roll noisily on steel tracks in the middle of the street.

A traffic policeman stands on a pedestal in the center of the intersection. He is also my friend.

He wears a white hat with a black shiny visor. My white knitted cap, which many small children wear, is tightly tied under my chin. The traffic policeman has a white wide leather belt with a shiny buckle. His dark blue uniform is the same color as my coat. Across his chest, over one shoulder he wears a wide strap that holds his gun holster. I wish I had a belt and a strap like my policeman friend. His large white-cuffed leather gloves are the same color as the knitted ones I wear on my tiny hands. I wish my brown high shoes were black like his shiny black ones.

He raises his right hand to halt the traffic, waves his other hand, points at cars, and motions to them to pass. He halts traffic again and points to the crowd of pedestrians gathered at the curb telling them it is safe to cross. The people obey and move as he directs them. He is the boss. He is the king of the hill. I want to be like him, to be in charge.

I salute him and shout, *"Zdravo!" Hello!* He turns toward me, and returns my salute. He motions for me to come to him. My first thought is, "What did I do wrong?" But, the broad smile on his face tells me that it is OK. I dash towards him abandoning the sidewalk that I am normally forbidden to leave.

He asks me, "What is your name?"

"Lubo." I reply.

"Lubo, how would you like to direct traffic?"

I think of Fräulein, my stern Austrian governess who is constantly telling me what to do, where to go, when to finish my meal, when to wash my hands, and when to be polite. I cannot believe that now I will be allowed to direct all those people and cars.

"You really mean it?" I ask.

He nods his head. "I will show you."

There is a lull in the traffic and my policeman friend teaches me how to direct the vehicles and people. To stop the traffic, I have to raise my right hand, palm facing the oncoming cars. To let them move again, I have to point my hand in the direction I want them to go and wave the other hand to usher them on.

I practice for a while. All this seems so easy, until several cars appear at the same time and my knees start to shake.

I am scared. I panic. "What do I do now?

Which hand do I raise first? Am I holding it right?"

I face a sea of cars and extend my hand, palm forward.

"Amazing!" The cars halt and I turn to let the car on my right go. As the car passes me, the driver smiles and waves. I look up and see that my policeman friend is imitating my moves. He tells me "Let the next car go." I point my hand in his direction and wave my other hand, letting him know that he can go. "Wow! What fun! The cars obey all my commands."

After the traffic slows down, my policeman friend shakes my hand and congratulates me on a job well done. Beaming from ear to ear, I face him, click my heels, and give him a snappy salute. He winks and salutes back. I turn on my heels and march like a real soldier, swinging my arms, and raising my feet high, back to Kolega on the sidewalk. I step onto the curb, swiftly turn around, and salute the policeman again. He returns my salute.

I am so proud. I glance up and see that Kolega is proud of me as well. I can't wait to tell mother, how I directed the traffic all by myself.

When I grow up, I too, will be a traffic policeman.

The Barber

Kolega and I join the crowd and continue down the street.

A rotating barber pole, the red and white stripes continuously climbing up, juts from the gray building next to a glass door with an "OPEN" sign hanging in the middle. Kolega opens the door. We enter. The air is filled with the smell of violets, soap, wet hair, and stale cigarettes.

Against one wall are four sinks and counters covered with white towels. Lined like pieces on a chessboard are: jars, bottles, tubes, brushes, and soap dishes. In the middle sits the King - a folded razor, and the Queen - a slim pair of pointed scissors.

Facing the counters are four white cast iron chairs with brown leather cushions. Four barbers, their white coat pockets filled with black combs, click their scissors like castanets over their customer's heads.

Waiting their turn several customers sit on the chairs on the other side of the room. Their faces are hidden behind large wicker newspaper holders they hold in their hands. Others stare at the illustrations in small weekly magazines. We join them and sit on two empty chairs against the wall.

I spot Toma, our barber. He grins. His white teeth sparkle under a stiff black mustache, tips pointing to each of his ears. His pomaded hair resembles a glistening black helmet. He looks evil. I am afraid of him. I don't like him.

"Oh, my next victim is here!" He roars as the customer gets off the chair. "NEXT!" He looks at me.

My bottom is glued to my chair. Kolega picks me up and places me on the wooden board, stretched over the chair's armrests.

Toma shakes a white apron with a loud clap and fastens it tightly around my neck. He is preparing me for my execution.

Toma chatters along as his scissors click around my ears. "Today my hand slipped and I cut one customer on the neck and the other on the cheek."

I cannot believe that I am sitting in the grips of this torturer. I imagine blood streaming from customers' faces, necks, and throats.

"Not a good day!" he continues.

Next, I feel something warm oozing behind my ears and the back of my neck. *Oh my God! Am I bleeding? Did he cut me?*

But I am relieved as I realize that it is only the warm soapsuds spreading across my neck.

Toma stretches the wide leather strap attached to the chair and raises the razor high in the air. With smooth strokes he slides the blade back and forth across the leather surface, turning it over with each stroke.

"Boy, today was really a bad day," he says. "I slipped and actually cut off a customer's whole ear."

Sweat beads form on my forehead.

"We had to get a needle and thread and sew it back on."

Kolega giggles in the background.

I imagine my ear flying through the air and jets of blood gushing out of the open wound.

Should I chance it?

I look at Toma's mustache, his shiny black hair, his evil grin, and the hand that holds the weapon.

This is it.

I jump off the chair to save my life. Suds fly from my ears; my protective cape sways behind me. I dash to freedom out the door. I run through the busy street. The barber runs behind. He holds the razor high above his head. Kolega runs behind him, laughing. I run down the street to the intersection where my policeman friend stands. I know he will save me.

People, on both sides of the street, stop and laugh.

Some yell, "Run! Run faster! Get away from that monster."

My little legs propel me as fast as they can, but are no match for Kolega, who overtakes the barber and swoops me up into his arms.

He laughs. I cry, as tears trickle down my face. He hugs me. He pulls my face close to his to comfort me, as soapsuds mixed with my tears wash down his cheek.

Lou Pechi

Mirče

Kolega takes me back to the barbershop and cleans me up. We leave and continue walking on the busy street. We go to a small café with display windows full of neat rows of small colorful Marzipan fruits, birthday cakes, various pastry, bonbons, and chocolate bars. The jingle of a tiny bell on the door announces us. We enter. I smell a strong chocolate and coffee smell, and hear the buzz of lively conversation. The mirrors on the wall reflect the faces of the people seated around marble-top tables full of saucers with coffee cups overflowing with mounds of whipped cream. Colorful desserts, and chocolate cakes dot each table. We find a small round table and Kolega asks me, "Do you want an Indianer?"

I nod, "Yes, of course."

An Indianer is a puffed pastry, filled with whipped cream and topped by a smooth glaze of chocolate. The shiny glaze reminds me of Toma's black pomaded hair. The sweet and smooth filling softens my image of the barber with his weapon.

We leave the café and walk through the park to our house on Zvonimirova Street, a wide boulevard with trolley tracks in the middle, surrounded by a fence of low green hedges. Our apartment is on the first floor. It has two entry doors. One door we hardly use leads to Kolega's office, and the other opens into a large entry hall where we eat our everyday meals. The bright room next to it is used only for guests. It faces the long outside balcony where my toy hobbyhorse Malen waits for me. His black mane waves in the morning breeze. I take off my coat and hat, put on my play clothes, and rush out to mount Malen. I pretend we are off galloping down the boulevard. Malen knows the way as the buildings zoom by.

Down below in the street I see the gypsy boy who walks by almost every day. He wears old tattered clothes. His hair is matted and the face smudged with dirt. I wave at him. He looks up and waves back. We never talk to each other. I don't even know his name.

At dinner that evening, I ask mother, whom I always call by the diminutive, Mutika.

"There is a gypsy boy, my age, who walks below our balcony every day. Could I play with him sometime?"

"Sure, you may," she says.

The next day instead of riding Malen I wait for the boy downstairs. He approaches, a smile on his face until he looks up. When he doesn't see me on the balcony his smile turns to a sad expression. I call out for him from the doorway and the bright smile returns to his smudged face.

"Hi! What is your name?" I ask him.

"Mirče," he says.

"I am Lubo. My name means love. Does your name mean anything?"

"Yes. It means peace."

"I think we will be good friends, because my full name, 'Ljubomir,' means lover of peace."

"How old are you?" I ask him.

He just shrugs his shoulders.

Mirče is about as tall as I; we must be the same age.

"Did you have breakfast?" I ask.

"No." He smirks, as if this was a stupid question. I guess he never eats breakfast.

"Well then, would you like to join us?"

He smiles and eagerly nods "Yes."

I call up to Mutika. "Can I invite my new friend Mirče for breakfast?"

"Of course," she answers.

We go up to our apartment and Mutika takes one look at my friend and starts the water running in the bathtub.

"Before we have breakfast we will give you a bath. Let's take off these old clothes," she tells him.

Mutika strips Mirče's clothing and he steps into the bathtub. She shampoos his hair, soaps a washcloth and scrubs him clean. His wet hair turns a shiny black and the smudges on his face melt into the bathtub water turning it a milky grey. He comes out and Mutika wraps him in a big towel. She dresses him in some of my clothes. They fit him perfectly. Mutika combs his hair. I can hardly recognize my new friend.

We have breakfast and I show him how to rock and ride Malen.

He tells me, "My father has two horses that pull our caravan. I ride them almost every day." I am impressed. When I grow up I will have a real horse.

We go inside and play with my toys.

"I don't have any toys," Mirče tells me.

I feel sorry for him. The morning goes by very quickly and Mirče has to go home. Mutika packs some of my shirts, pants, underwear, and a pair of my shoes into a paper bag. I add a small truck that Mirče liked.

We say goodbye and Mirče leaves.

The next day I eagerly await Mirče, but he does not show up. Days go by and there is no sign of him. I liked having a friend. "What happened?"

Several weeks later, after I gave up on Mirče, he appears on the sidewalk below. He wears his old torn clothes. His hair is matted and face smudged with dirt; his left eye is black and blue. I wave at him. He lowers his head and does not look at me. He briefly waves his hand in my direction, and walks away without looking back.

I run to Mutika, tears in my eyes. I don't understand. "What did I do?"

She sits me down and explains. "Mirče is a Gypsy boy. His father makes him beg on the streets. If he is dressed in fine clothes with his hair neatly combed, people would not feel sorry for him, and nobody would give him any money."

"Does his father beat him?" I ask.

"Why?" She asks.

"Because, I saw that he has a black and blue eye."

"His father probably beat him to make him beg."

Why does Mirče's father make him beg? It is not

fair! Why does he beat him? My Kolega does not make me beg. He never hit me. I am so lucky to have him as my father. He is a real Kolega.

Lou Pechi

The Toy Train

Kolega sometimes travels on business to Germany, Austria, and Italy. I don't like when he leaves and can't wait until he comes back. He always brings me back candy and chocolates, and what I like even better, windup cars and mechanical toys. Many of the toys are made from painted tin, held together by tiny bent tabs.

I love to wind them up by the key that sticks out of the side and watch them go around. I am careful not to overwind them. Once, I forced the key and the spring came loose with a loud noise that scared me. I decided to fix the toy. With a butter knife I pried open the small tabs and split the toy into two half shells. I found where the spring came off and forced it into position. Holding on to just the motor, I carefully wound the key and watched the gears spring into action; the big slow moving gear, connected to the mainspring, meshed to the ever-smaller faster moving gears that drive the wheels.

My favorites are the SCHUCO toy cars. They are very sturdy and come with a separate silver key with a square hole on its end. The key matches a square windup-pin inside the small hole on the side of the car. The toy car looks real since I can remove the key, before letting the car run. I don't like the other cars where I can't remove the key. Also I don't have to worry about over-winding the SCHUCO cars because their spring slides without ever popping off. The most fascinating car Kolega brings me is the one that runs on the dining room table without falling off. I wonder how the car knows to turn when it reaches the rim.

Kolega points and explains. "See the four wheels that make the car go straight. Behind the front two wheels is this hidden wheel pointing in the other direction. Well, when the front two wheels go off the edge, that wheel touches the table and steers the car away from the edge."

I don't fully understand how it works, but I am happy that my Kolega understands how it works.

One day he returns with a big box. "Guess what is in it?" he asks.

"A big windup toy car?"

"No, Lubo. It is a whole electric train set!"

He starts pulling out curved and straight railroad tracks. He attaches them together to form a big oval, connects them to a black transformer and control box, and plugs the power cord into the wall socket. Next he places a black locomotive, a small tender, and several brown railroad cars on the tracks.

"OK. Ready to roll," he says as he slowly turns the crank on the control box. The front light of the locomotive shines brightly and the train slowly begins to move.

"Can I run the train?"

"Of course. It is your train." Kolega shows me how to make the train go forward and back up. I spend the rest of the evening transporting my toys from one end of the room to the other. Within the next few weeks I add more tracks and transport cubes of sugar, salt, and pepper from the kitchen to my mother, my dear Mutika, who sits at the table in the dining room.

Lou Pechi

The Incident

My governess, who I call Fräulein, takes me to the park almost every day. She was born in a small Austrian village and speaks to me in German. Fräulein always wears a short-sleeved gray dress, buttoned up to her neck and a long-sleeved black jacket that she takes off when it gets too hot. She carries a big black leather purse from which, like from a magician's hat, she can pull anything she or I need: handkerchiefs, combs, brushes, sandwiches, and even an occasional toy. Her heavy black shoes make a clicking sound when she walks.

Each day Mutika wears a different colorful dress and matching high heel shoes that make her look very tall. Her reddish-brown hair is always nicely combed. Her long fingernails are painted a shiny red. Once a week she goes to the hairdresser to have her hair and nails done. I love to watch her as she darkens her eyebrows with a highlighter pencil, puckers her lips to put on shiny red lipstick, and curls her eyelashes with an eyelash-curler. Mutika is seldom home and when she is gone, I try to use the eyelash-curler on my eyelashes. Mutika spends a lot of time in the big coffeehouse downtown with her friends. In the evenings she goes to nightclubs and fancy balls with Kolega. I spend most of my time with Fräulein, whom I don't like very much. I would rather be with Mutika.

Fräulein's greyish hair, slicked down, pulled into a bun in the back of her head, matches the dull color of her dress. She never wears makeup and seldom smiles. Her fingernails are cut short and she never paints them.

Every day Fräulein takes me to the local park where she meets her boyfriend Oscar. Oscar is usually late and Fräulein sits and waits on a bench under the trees. She constantly looks at her watch. Oscar is late today. Whenever Oscar does come, they sit close together and he puts his arm around her shoulder. They stare at each other and whisper something to each other. *For me this is so boring!*

I go and play in the sand box, commanding a squadron of tin soldiers ready to attack the fort on the other mound of sand.

"Load your muskets! Attach your bayonets! Advance! Fire!" I shout.

The explosions, created by my fists, scatter the enemy soldiers. Tin fighters advance one by one shooting their tiny muskets. I shout, "BANG, BANG! BOOM!"

Suddenly I feel a pressure in my tummy. I have to go to the bathroom. I declare a truce, leave the soldiers in their battle positions, and run to Fräulein.

"I have to go ca-ca real bad."

"Hold it in. You will have to wait. Oscar will be here any minute now."

I return to my soldiers, but have no will to command them. I try to hold the pressure in, but the urge is too strong. I am not a baby anymore. I am proud that I can use the bathroom by myself whenever I have to go. And this time I really have to go.

"I can't hold it in."

"Hold it in. I told you already. We can't leave now," she says, her face distorted in an angry scowl.

Dancing from foot to foot, tears start to form in my eyes and I scream,

"I CAN'T HOLD IT IN ANYMORE!"

My bowels explode. Brown warmth fills my pants. A strong stinky smell fills the air and shame overcomes me. She pulls me by my hand and drags me into the doorway of our apartment house.

"I told you to hold it in!" Fraulein hits me on my back, carefully avoiding my swollen bottom. I do not cry. The blows don't hurt me; my pride does.

She clenches her teeth and pulls me by my hand into the bathroom. My shoulder hurts. I whimper softly. "I can take it. I am a big boy. I am almost four and a half."

I don't want to give her the satisfaction of crying. Fräulein beats me frequently, but I never cry or complain. I accept the blows quietly. I never tell my parents.

"I told you to hold it in," she repeats for the fourth time. "You should have held it in."

The words bounce off the shiny bathroom tiles. She turns on the bathtub faucet. I listen to the splash of the water and tune her out. She turns the water off, takes my shoes off, and tells to me to step into the tub. *Isn't she going to remove my clothes and clean me up before I take my bath?*

As soon as I am in the bathtub, she strips my clothes and dumps them in the water. The smell of wet clothes and floating brown stuff fills the air. I sit, in rage, surrounded by brown turds, my own ca-ca bobbing in the murky stinking water around me.

I hate her. How could she do this to me? It was not my fault. I couldn't help it. I told her in time. Why did she have to wait for Oscar? Why? Why? Why?

The next day at breakfast I announce to my parents," I don't want to see Fräulein again."

"Why? What happened?" Kolega and Mutika ask at once.

"Because I hate her. I don't mind if she hits me all the time. But, I don't want her to put me in the tub with my soiled clothes ever again." I am angry.

"What do you mean? Slow down. Start from the beginning." Kolega puts his hand on my shoulder.

I sob. "Yesterday, when we went to the park, I had to go to the bathroom, but Fräulein wouldn't leave. We had to wait for Oscar. I couldn't hold it in and made ca-ca in my pants. She beat me and put me in the bathtub with my clothes on. I hate her."

Both Kolega and Mutika embrace me.

"Don't worry about a thing. We will take care of you."

The next day Fräulein is gone and Mutika takes me to the park. I am happy.

Juan Les Pins

For our vacation that summer, instead of going to the beach at Crikvenica, on the coast of Croatia, we go to Juan Les Pins in France. Kolega has to stay in Zagreb. He has too much work to do. A long train ride and a short taxi ride bring my mother and me to our pension in Juan Les Pins late the same afternoon. A large white villa, hidden behind several tall pine trees faces the blue Mediterranean. A portly old lady in a black button down dress and a white apron around her ample waist opens the door. Her hair is a tangle of grey curls. Her glasses dangle on her big chest from a string around her neck. She welcomes us with a big smile on her face.

"Bienvenue à la Maison Dubois. Je suis Madame Dubois." I don't understand anything she says. French is such a funny sounding language.

"I am Madame Peći and this is my son Lubo." Mutika points a finger at herself and then to me.

"Tu es un charmant petit garçon," as the old lady pinches my cheek.

"I am Lubo." I insist.

"Je suis enchantée, petit garçon," she answers, ignoring my real name.

"I am Lubo," I repeat, but she ignores me, and for the rest of our stay insists on calling me, "Petit garcon."

All I understand is "petit" which to me

sounds like Croatian number five — "Pet".

It must be that in France instead of using my name they use my age.

We follow her and climb a marble staircase to our room. She opens the shutters to the balcony and through the pine trees in the front yard, I can see the beach and the blue sea that stretches as far as the eye can see.

A white tent hangs above each bed.

"Why do they have tents over the beds?" I ask Mutika.

She laughs. "Those are not tents, Lubo. Those are mosquito nets. They keep the mosquitos away so that they will not bite you while you sleep."

"Can I climb into the net?"

"Go ahead, but take your shoes off first."

I climb under the transparent mesh and spread the bottom edges to form a large space. I pretend that I am camping in Africa, like the explorers in the scary movie Fräulein took me to in Zagreb. I feel safe and cozy inside, as lions and tigers circle around. They can't harm me. Mutika lifts one side and I panic, afraid.

"No. No. Close the flap. Don't let the lions and the tigers in."

"Let me just put on your pajamas, and you can go back." She laughs and puts on my pajamas and I quickly scoot under the blankets into the safety of my tent. I fall asleep as the lions and tigers circle.

The next morning we join Uncle Milan and Aunt Anika, our close friends, for breakfast in the back garden of the villa; they arrived from Zagreb the night before. Birds in the flowering bushes chirp in harmony with a half dozen finches in a large cage suspended from one of the villa's arches. Madame Dubois brings two plates with eggs standing up in white holders.

"Why do they put eggs in little cups?" I ask, never having been served eggs in their shells.

"Those are soft boiled eggs. That is how they serve them in France. Here, I will show you how to eat them." Mutika taps the top of the shell with her knife and lifts the round top off. She sprinkles some salt and hands me a small spoon. I scoop the soft insides and eat it with the freshly baked and buttered brioches.

"Yummy! I like soft-boiled eggs. They are so good." I am delighted.

The adults drink their black coffee and I taste my milk.

"I don't like plain milk. Can I please have some Ovaltine?"

"We don't have any Ovaltine here. Let me put some sugar in and pour a bit of black coffee. It will taste just like Ovaltine." Mutika reassures me, but when I taste the light brown milk, it doesn't taste like Ovaltine at all. I drink it anyway. Drinking coffee makes me feel like a grownup.

After breakfast we go to our room and I put on my bathing suit and my terry robe. Mutika puts on her long housecoat over her bathing suit.
We meet in the lobby and notice that Uncle Milan is still wearing his pajamas.

"Why are you still wearing your pajamas? Are you not going to the beach with us?" I ask Uncle Milan.

"I *am* going with you. I already have my bathing suit under the pajamas. That way I don't have to use the dressing room," he says.

I think this is so funny and start to laugh. I point my finger at him. "Ha! Ha! You can't wear pajamas on the street. You can't wear pajamas on the street."

Everybody laughs. But he does wear his pajamas anyway.

We carry our blankets in a big canvas bag and walk along the boulevard to the beach. Palm trees line one side of the street. The beach on the other side is bordered by a row of lampposts on concrete pillars, connected by cast iron grating fence. We go down the steps and spread our blanket on the soft sand. Mutika smears suntan lotion on me before I run to the water and splash in the waves. I am careful not to go too deep in the water. I don't know how to swim yet. Before I realize it, Mutika calls me for lunch.

"Just a bit more," I protest. "I am having so much fun."

Eventually I join everyone on the blanket and eat my sandwich. A dark suntanned man with a large straw hat walks along the beach shouting, "Pédalo". Pédalo. Pédalo." I start to laugh. To me it sounds like "Budalo," which in Croatian means, "Stupid."

"Budalo!" Uncle Milan shouts to the man. I

laugh and join him shouting, "Budalo, Budalo." It is so much fun calling an older man stupid.

The man approaches us. Not speaking French the man extends all five fingers on his hand. Uncle Milan extends three fingers. The man shakes his head from side to side and extends only four fingers. Uncle Milan nods and pays the man with four crisp notes. We follow him to a row of double-hulled boats. A bench is mounted on a plank connecting the hulls, and two sets of pedals connect to a paddle wheel in the middle. Uncle Milan lifts me onto the bench, but I am too small to reach the pedals. The man pushes the boat into the water.

Uncle Milan points to a lever between us. "Lubo, why don't you steer and I will pedal. If you move the lever to the left the boat will go to the right and if you move it to the right it will go left."

Uncle Milan pedals and we start to move forward. We start to go left and then right as I move the lever to each side.

"Hold the lever steady in the middle," Uncle Milan tells me.

I do and soon learn how to control where we go. I am so proud that I can steer the boat. The "Budalo" man on the beach waves his hands at us, signaling our time is up. I steer the boat toward the beach. We were out such a short time.

"Can we rent the boat tomorrow again?" I ask uncle Milan.

"We will see." He smiles.

We pack our gear and walk back to our pension for my afternoon nap. I shower and climb under my tent, which now magically transforms into a boat that I steer in a jungle river. I float down the river. Lions and tigers play on the shores. Black natives, spears in their hands, peek behind the bushes. I feel safe on my boat and shut my eyes as I fall asleep.

I wake up as Mutika gently touches my cheek, "It's time to get up for dinner. Dress up."

We join our friends in the back garden. Several other occupants of the hotel already sit at round metal tables covered with white tablecloths.
I can smell chicken soup, my favorite. Madame Dubois approaches our table with a tray full of teacups. She picks one up, places it in my soup plate and upturns it to pour the chicken soup. I have never seen anyone pour soup like she does. They do everything differently in France. In Zageb our maid Maritza serves the soup already in my plate, and when I am done and uncover the rooster design on the bottom I crow, "Kuku-Riku!"

After dinner, the adults sit around the table, smoke their cigarettes and drink wine. I am bored and not interested in their conversation. I find a quiet spot in the garden and play with my soldiers until Mutika puts me to bed for the night.

Our first day and all the others in Juan Les Pins are much the same and wonderful for me. My pale skin changes to a healthy tan and my brown hair turns blond. Before I know it is time to return to Zagreb.

Kindergarten

After we return from our vacation, Mutika tells me, "Now that summer is over you will be starting Kindergarten."

"What is Kindergarten?"

"It is like going to school."

I am worried about being left alone. I still think of Fräulein, and how she beat me. "Will you stay with me?" I ask Mutika.

My mother reassures me. "No. I will take you there and pick you up. You will be with many children your age."

I feel better that I will be with other children.

The Montessori Kindergarten is on the second floor of a building behind the Central Market. We cross the market. Large tables, shaded by big red umbrellas, are lined in rows. They overflow with multicolored fruit: apples, strawberries, pears, peaches, grapes, tomatoes, peppers, onions, cabbages, and parsley. Their fresh scents blend with the fragrant bunches of colorful spring flowers in buckets of water on the ground.

Older peasant women in multicolored embroidered dresses, red kerchiefs on their heads, stand behind each table and hawk their wares in shrill voices.

"Get my beautiful apples!"

"Juicy tomatoes, Picked this morning!"

"Straaawberries!"

I like the familiar market and would rather

linger there. Holding Mutika's hand we climb to the second floor of the building facing the market. Two doors greet us: one with a painted sign "English Montessori", the other with "French Montessori." We enter the English one. Several small coats hang on colorful racks against the wall, children's hats on the top shelves and little red rubber boots on the bottom ones. Each shelf is marked with a decal of an animal. A stern lady— her gray hair piled high on her head, eyeglasses dangling on her chest by a chain — greets us with a sugary sweet smile. She wears a long grey dress and low-heeled black shoes that remind me of Fräulein. I am wary. *I hope she is not as mean.*

"I am Mrs. Kovačić and I will be your teacher," she says.

"Pleased to meet you," I say, looking down at my shoes.

Mrs. Kovačić shows me a hook and shelf on the coat rack with a picture of a mouse. "This will be your place. You can take off your coat and hat and hang them there."

I don't like to take orders and reluctantly walk to my rack and place my coat on a hook under the little mouse. "He is cute. I like tiny mice. Maybe it won't be so bad," I whisper to myself, and smile.

She opens the door to a large room with several rows of small children's desks. They are lined just like the stands in the market, but there are no big red umbrellas on top and no hawkers behind them. Instead boys and girls my age sit and hold wooden frames in their hands. As we enter they lift their heads from the frames and look at me. They seem to wonder who the new boy is, while I am fascinated by the wooden frames and try to figure out what they are. Mrs. Kovačić picks a frame from the shelf and hands it to me. She puts her hand on my shoulder, and leads me to my desk. I see that the frame has two fabric panes with a row of holes on each end, just like the lace holes on my shoes. She gives me a long shoelace and shows me how to thread it through the holes and tie a big bow on the end. During what feels like forever, we thread the shoelaces through the holes, tie the bow, untie the bow, unlace, thread, tie, untie, unlace, until lunch finally frees us from our boring labor.

After lunch, Mrs. Kovačić gives each one of us a large illustrated book with black lettered short sentences on the bottom of each page. Mrs. Kovačić explains that before we start learning English, we need to learn how to read in our own Croatian language. I already know how to read and start turning the pages to finish the story.

Mrs. Kovačić interrupts my reading:

"Lubo, you are not supposed to go ahead of every body else. You don't know how to read yet. We all need to read together and point our little fingers to each word we read."

"But, I know how to read already."

"That can't be true," she argues.

"I can read!" I am angry that she does not believe me. "My Kolega taught me all the letters on his big black typewriter in his office."

To show her, I start reading the story aloud.

"That is very good," Mrs. Kovačić says. "You seem to be ready to learn English."

She takes me by my hand and leads me to a group of children sitting around a young lady. "Miss Gold, this is Lubo, our new student. He already knows how to read."

Miss Gold is pretty. She wears a blue smock. Her blond hair falls down to her shoulders. Her blue eyes sparkle under thin dark brown eyebrows. She has smooth rosy cheeks and lips painted with a bright red lipstick.

"Why don't you join us?" She points to an empty seat in the circle and smiles at me. I like her right away and am happy to be in her class and away from Mrs. Kovačić.

Miss Gold raises a flash card from a pile on the desk and clearly pronounces the word in English.

We repeat: "Shoe, Duck, Pencil, Hat, Dog, Cat," as each parades, one after the other, in front of our eyes and we pronounce the words in this strange English language.

Over the next several months, the dogs on the flash cards start to bark, the cats to meow, the children to walk, go to school, and greet each other.

"Hello, what is your name? I am John."

They start to introduce their brothers, sisters, and uncles, describe their homes, estates, villages, and cities.

All of us in turn, start talking to Miss Gold in our new adopted language.

My family is proud of my English. When my

parents' friends come over for dinner they want to show them what I learned in Kindergarten and ask me to say something in English.

"How do you do?" I say.

My parents' friends mimic me "Do, do, do." and laugh. I laugh with them and think how really silly they are.

Lou Pechi

To Belgrade

Mutika tells me: "Next week the Kindergarten will be closed for Passover and Easter. We are going to Belgrade to visit your grandfather Apuci, and your uncles Laci and Marci."

I am happy. I love my grandfather. Going to Belgrade by train will be so much fun.

The next day, Kolega loads our suitcases into the trunk of our car and takes us to the railroad station. The platform is crowded with people carrying luggage of various sizes and shapes. Kolega calls a porter who takes our suitcases to our compartment on the train, and lifts the bags onto the racks above. Kolega pays him, gives Mutika a kiss, hugs me in a strong embrace and kisses me on both cheeks. He is not coming with us. He has to report to the military. Kolega leaves the train and I, standing on my tippy toes, watch him through the glass window, waving to us on the platform. The window is too tall and Mutika picks me up. I lean over and I wave back. There is a loud whistle, a big puff of steam from the engine, and the train starts to move.

Kolega walks and then runs on the platform to keep with us. As the train speeds up, he stops and continues waving. The train speeds ahead and he fades into a tiny speck. Mutika puts me down and we enter our compartment. I miss him already. Without him the thrill of traveling by train is gone. I sit on the padded seat by the window and fall asleep to the rocking and the rhythmic clanging of the train wheels. Six hours later we arrive in Belgrade.

I see Uncle Laci waiting for us in the brightly lit station. He kisses Mutika and lifts me high up in the air.

"My how you have grown. And, how heavy you are!"

Uncle Laci is the father of my cousin Freddy whom we all call "Bubi." Though he is just a few years older than me, Bubi already wears long pants. When he visits us I love to play with him under our dining room table.

Uncle Laci calls a porter, who helps us load our luggage onto a taxi waiting in front of the station. I look in awe as we drive through the streets of Belgrade. At night the city sparkles like a jewel. Lamp posts, lit building windows, bright store windows with mannequins dressed in fancy clothes, cafés full of people who talk and sip their drinks light our way to my uncle's apartment.

We take the elevator to the second floor. Apuci opens the door, picks me up, and holds me to his soft big belly. He smells of cigars. He laughs, and in his deep voice greets me by my diminutive: "Ho! Ho! Ho! Here is my Ljubče."

He reminds me of Santa Claus with dark hair and no beard.

He puts me down and shows us our bedroom. Mutika unpacks our suitcase, helps me into my pajamas and tucks me into bed. I still miss my Kolega, but I feel safe with my kind and jolly uncles.

I am very tired, and quickly fall asleep.

Lou Pechi

STORMY

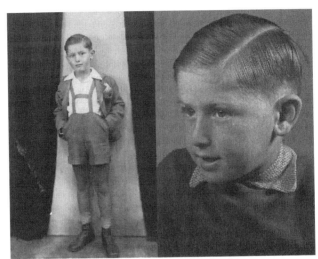

Brod – Confirmation **Brod –** Lubo

Zagreb – Srečko

Lou Pechi

Belgrade

Belgrade, early morning Sunday, April 6, 1941

I dream that I am floating on my back, arms stretched out, down a slow moving river. The waves softly rock me as I gaze at the white clouds above. The clouds start to move more quickly, blown by wind. I realize that I am moving faster down the stream. The river starts to pick up speed. The water turns choppy. I hear the thundering rumble of a waterfall ahead. I panic. I try to swim upstream. The strong current pulls me over the edge. I plunge to the deep bottom. I can't breathe. I am drowning. Gasping for air I awaken with a start to find myself lying in my bed.

I sit up, and listen. A strange buzzing sound, like a nest of angry hornets, is coming from outside. I wonder, "What is making all that noise?"

I put on my slippers and run to the balcony outside.

I grab the cold railing with both hands and look up. The early morning sky is clear. The strange sound is coming from the horizon, where the blue meets the gray outline of the city. It is filled with black specs moving toward me. The tiny dots move closer and grow bigger. They start to resemble flocks of blackbirds in the 'V' formations of migrating geese. As they get closer I realize that they are not birds, but shiny airplanes.

I never saw so many airplanes at one time.

"Where did they come from? What are they doing here?"

One of the planes tilts its wings and, like an eagle spotting its prey below, dives toward the ground. The others follow, accompanied by the earsplitting shriek of sirens.

I cover my ears and run back in, colliding with the open arms of Uncle Laci. I feel safe in his big, warm body's embrace.

"What is the matter, Lubo? What is going on?"

"The planes are falling from the sky. They are screaming for help. They will crash."

Grandpa Apuci, Mutika, and Uncle Marci shuffle onto the small balcony and look up. The planes continue to dive, still accompanied by the wailing siren.

"They must be ours. Just practicing," Uncle Laci says.

"The air-raid sirens didn't sound." Apuci observes.

"Can you see their markings?" Mutika asks.

"Crosses. Oh my God, they are not ours. They are German." Laci responds. "Turn on the radio."

Mutika goes into the room and turns on the radio. We hear Édith Piaf singing "La Vie En Rose."

"This can't be an emergency broadcast," my mother says.

"Look, they are dropping bombs," I shout when I notice black shapes dropping from the airplanes' bellies, followed by booming explosions.

Each bang feels like a punch in my belly. My ears clog up. I can barely hear Uncle Laci yelling, "Everybody down to the cellar."

He is a reserve captain in the Royal Yugoslav Defense Army. He knows what to do.

"Let me at least get dressed," Mutika protests.

"*No!* We don't have time. Everybody down to the basement. *Now!*" Uncle Laci repeats.

Mutika heads toward the elevator.

Laci stops her. "*No! No!* Not the elevator! The stairs."

We follow him down the dark stairway. As we open the door to the basement, we see eyes filled with terror peeking from the darkness of the cellar. I get used to the darkness. As my eyes adjust to the darkness I see huddles of our neighbors, blankets draped over their heads, their faces frozen in horror. We find a space against a wall and sit on the ground.

Bomb blasts shake the ground. It feels like riding over bumps in a car. I hold my breath, afraid to exhale. I await each blast, praying it is the last one. Children scream. Parents embrace them more tightly.

Men shout, "Don't panic! Stay down!"

Another loud explosion sends a wall of coal on the other side of the room tumbling down. A cloud of black dust fills the air. I scream, but no one can hear me. I sit still, too scared to move, waiting for the next blast. But, there is only silence.

The attack ends just as quickly as it began.

The coal dust slowly settles to the floor. All is quiet.

"Is it over?" I whisper. "I have to make pee-pee."

Uncle Laci still embraces me and answers "Let's go outside, I think it is safe by now."

We cautiously walk through the fallen rubble by the door and climb up the steps to the entrance of the building. All is still. The house across the street, beautiful the day before, is split like an open dollhouse. The contents of half a kitchen hang dangerously on a slanting floor. A sink is suspended in mid air by its pipes. A bed dangles, at an odd angle, from the remnants of a bedroom. Flames and smoke sprout from the windows of the building next door.

In front of our house, a stiff horse, hooves in the air, still hitched to the overturned cart, spills its red and purple guts on the pavement. No one looks at him. People walk by as if lost in a dream. Everyone seems to be looking for someone or something, no one understanding, or believing the horror in front of their dazed eyes.

I relieve myself against the wall of our building. My eyes are fixed on the dead horse. I can't stop looking at his open bulging eyes. I think of my hobbyhorse Malen in Zagreb. Uncle Laci reaches over and gently turns my head away. His touch sends a shiver through my body.

I start sobbing. My pee streams again, in irregular spurts.

Escape from Belgrade

Her hair tied in a bandana above her forehead, a rucksack firmly on her shoulder, Mutika holds my hand as we make our way to the Belgrade railroad station to catch the train home to Zagreb.

The station is crowded with people waiting. We hear the slow chugging, see smoke blowing from the chimney, steam swooshing from its sides as a train pulls into the station. People run to the doors and push each other as they try to get in.

"Save two seats for you and your mom," Uncle Laci says as he lifts me and pushes me headfirst through the open window of a railroad car.

I land on my hands on the hard wooden bench and stretch my body across the seats. The bench reeks of unwashed feet, sweaty armpits, greasy hair under peasant hats or women's scarves, all mixed with the pungent smell of stale tobacco.

The compartment door opens and people, pushed from behind, flow in, like water gushing over a dam.

"Move over!" they scream as they try to squeeze me into a tight bundle. I resist.

"These are our seats!"

"I am saving them for my mom," I shout, tears welling in my eyes.

Mutika appears in the doorway and sits next to me as I swing my legs down and she can finally sit in my seat. I feel good. I am only six years old, but I saved two seats.

The engine emits a loud hoot, the compartment jerks, and the train starts to move away from Belgrade and toward Zagreb. As it picks up speed, telephone poles pass the window and quicken their tempo. The city fades, replaced by green fields and trees. Coats are unbuttoned, hats removed, and smiles replace serious looks as stiff bodies relax. Baskets of food appear, checkered red cloths are spread on laps, and the smell of fresh bread, bacon, and fried chicken fills the small compartment.

"What a cute little boy. What is your name?" A heavyset peasant woman asks me.

"I am Lubo" I reply.

"What a nice name. Where are you going to?"

"We are trying to return to Zagreb" Mutika replies.

She offers us some of the fried chicken and fresh bread. Mutika gratefully accepts and takes two small pieces. Mutika gives me a chicken leg. I love fried chicken.

Gradually everyone joins the conversation, and the same people, who previously fought each other for the few empty seats, get to know each other, become friends, and one family. Our hunger satisfied, conversation subsides, and sleep overtakes us. I climb up on the baggage rack above the seats and stretch out. From my high perch above, as if flying, I watch the people below and the passing scenery through the window. Time passes quickly and we approach another Serbian provincial town.

A screech of brakes, a few jerks, and the train comes to a stop. A fat stationmaster holds a red flag and announces in a loud voice:

"Please everyone exit the train. This train is not going any further. The Germans blew up the bridge over river Sava this morning."

"Where are we?" my mother asks the conductor.

"Ruma" he replies.

Mutika is puzzled. "Ruma?" Suddenly her face brightens.

"I know someone in this town. Erika is the sister of my best friend Anika. She is married to Willy Schlesinger. His parents live in Ruma. Maybe we can stay with them."

We pick up our backpacks and Mutika approaches the stationmaster. "We are looking for the family Schlesinger. Do you know them?"

"Yes, as a matter of fact. They are good friends of mine. They live nearby. Just follow this street to a yellow house, number 27." He points to the street on the right of the train station.

A short way down the street we knock on the door of the yellow house. An elderly gentleman opens the door and smiles at us:

"Pirika!" That is Mutika's real name. "What a surprise. What are you doing in Ruma?"

"We are on our way to Zagreb from Belgrade. The Germans bombed the tracks ahead. Would it be possible to stay with you?"

"Of course. You are more than welcome.

Come on in. As it happens, Erika and Willy are here for the holidays." Mr. Schlesinger ushers us in.

Like long lost friends, everyone embraces and kisses each other. I don't like when they all start to hug me and plant their wet kisses. Mrs. Schlesinger adds two additional plates to the already set dinner table and we all sit down to eat. We are suddenly interrupted by shouts on the streets. I run to the window and peek behind the curtains. Groups of men in leather coats, hunting rifles on their shoulders, are roaming the streets. I see that they wear red armbands with a white round patch in the middle. In the center of the patch is a sign that looks like a black running cross. It is the same mark the German airplanes in Belgrade had on their sides.

"They are the "*Volksdeutsche*", the fifth column Nazi sympathizers." I overhear Mr. Shlesinger.

I see one of the men approach the house and begin angrily knocking on the front door. The dog chained in the back yard begins to bark, and the man at the door shouts, "Dirty Jews out!" He continues to bang loudly on the door.

I hide behind Mutika.

Mr. Schlesinger tells Willy, "Hurry. Go and hide inside the doghouse in the back yard and keep the dog in front of you. They will not look there."

Mr. Schlesinger opens the door. "There are only women and children in the house."

"Where is Willy?" They ask.

"He left last night for Zagreb" Willy's father

responds. "Go ahead, look through the house."

The men push past him and start looking under the bed. They open the cupboards in every room and, finally convinced that Willy is not there, they leave still yelling "We will get that dirty Jew yet."

We all stand still, eyes wide open, unable to talk or move, paralyzed by fear, paralyzed by the hate.

Mutika is the only one who speaks. "We have to leave."

"But, where can you go? How will you get past the mob on the street?" Mr. Schlesinger asks.

"Is there an exit through the back yard?" Mutika asks.

Mr. Schlesinger nods. "There is a gate in the back of the house that leads to the neighbor's yard and to another street."

We pack just what we can carry in our backpacks and say good-bye to everyone. Willy and Erika stay behind, and will rejoin us after we find out if there is a way to get out of town.

It is dark. I am afraid, but the comforting grip of Mutika's hand leads me through the back yard and the neighbor's vegetable garden as we exit to an empty street.

We reach the railroad station and find out from the station manager that the broken bridge is a few hours walk from the town. If we follow the tracks, we should be there by dawn. He says, "Only the tracks are damaged. You should be able to cross the bridge by foot."

We start walking on the tracks. I step from trestle to trestle, as my short strides perfectly match their spacing. Mutika trudges on the gravel, her shoes making a crunching sound with each step. I want to go to sleep. I am tired of walking. At the break of dawn we reach the bridge where there is a crowd. Peasant women wear colorful bandanas and their flowing skirts almost touch the ground. Men wear black hats, white shirts with flowing sleeves, and dark vests. Barefoot children play among large baskets on the ground.

One of the men speaks to Mutika. "It is too dangerous to cross the bridge. No one can get across."

He gazes across the river, as if by staring at the other bank he will be somehow transported to the other side.

"Is there another way to cross the river?" Mutika asks the man.

He turns his head. "Yes. A mile downstream is a barge crossing and for a fee of 50.00 Dinars, which is a fortune I don't have, you can cross the river."

"Thank you," my mother says.

We trudge along the banks until I see a rope stretched across the river and a barge moored on our side. Mutika bargains with the man on the barge who does not charge for me. We climb on the bobbing barge. I don't feel well. The motion of the barge, the lack of sleep, and the exhaustion make my tummy ache. I get sick and vomit over the edge into the flowing water. Mutika holds my head and wipes my face with a handkerchief she has soaked in the cold river.

The barge casts off, the rope strains to keep the barge from floating downstream. Finally we are on the other side. I feel better standing on solid ground.

We walk toward a small village. "I hope we can find an inn or a house where we can rest," Mutika says.

Villagers stand in doorways of shabby houses. They look at us as we trudge through the muddy street. By our clothes they can tell we are city folks and do not belong in their village.

Mutika inquires of one lady standing in her doorway. "Is there a house we could rest in?"

"No," the woman says, "but the lady in the house across the street sometimes rents her spare room."

We cross the street, and are shown in. Mutika bargains with the lady and shortly we are ushered into a small room with a large bed covered by a thick feather eiderdown. I run and leap onto it, sinking in as if it were fresh snow. It envelops me in its soft warmth. Mutika takes off my shoes and my backpack as I quickly drift into a long awaited sleep.

I wake up the next morning, now under the covers, wearing only my shorts and my t-shirt. Someone is gently shaking my shoulder. It is Mutika.

"Time to get up," she whispers. "We have to get going. There is a freight train leaving the station soon."

We start walking toward the station, as we munch on freshly baked bread our hostess gave us. I eat my piece slowly, savoring the crunchy crust and the soft warm center. The bread tastes so good.

A long freight train, its brown cars lined up behind the locomotive, stretches across the station platform. We climb onto one of the metal ladders attached to each brakeman's cabin that towers over each freight car. Several people already stand in the cabin and we barely manage to squeeze in. In the middle of the cabin is a round wheel used to apply the brakes to that car.

There is no place to sit, and so Mutika lifts me and sets me down on top of the wheel. I tower over the rest of the people as I sit like a king on my perch. I can see from one of the windows the freight cars behind ours and from another window in front the locomotive and freight cars ahead.

The engine emits several loud hoots and the train begins to move, picking up speed. A warm breeze blows into my face. Plowed fields, orchards, red roofed houses, cows in pastures, picket fences, follow each other. The pattern repeats until the scattered houses get closer to each other and their height increases. We are approaching the big city of Zagreb.

The train stops in the freight yard before reaching the main station. "This is a good place to get off," Mutika says. "It is much closer to our house. We can walk home."

The Intruders

Zagreb is aglow on this beautiful spring day. In the weeks since we left to visit my grandfather and uncles in Belgrade, the trees sprouted shiny new green leaves that seem to reflect the morning sun. It is good to be back home, wrapped in the familiar fresh green smell of the park where I used to play every day. At this early hour only a few people scurry through the empty streets; they are hunched over, staring at the path in front, absorbed in their morning thoughts. Mutika's hair is still bound in a red bandana tied above her forehead. She carries her rucksack as she holds my hand and we walk from the freight terminal to our apartment a few blocks away.

I look up to the balcony and see my hobby horse Malen patiently waiting. I am glad that I tied his reins to the balcony railing before we left our house two weeks ago. His black mane and tail wave in the light breeze, as if he is welcoming me back home. Malen is still, not rocking. He is waiting for me.

Mutika unlocks the front door of the apartment house and we climb the stairs to our apartment on the first floor. I run up to our door and ring the bell, eager to untie Malen and ride him.

A voice from behind the door asks, "Who is it?"

I recognize the voice of Maritza, our live-in maid, and answer "It's Lubo."

She opens the door, just as Mutika climbs the last step to our floor. After being gone for two weeks I expect Maritza to hug and pick me in her arms and cover me with kisses, but she just stands there, a frightened look on her face. I look back at Mutika and see the same worry reflected in her face. What is wrong?

"Madam," Maritza tells us, her voice quaking. "There are two German officers in your bedroom." She leans her head closer to Mutika and whispers into her ear. "I *had* to let them in."

Mutika's face turns white and loses all expression. I don't like that look on her face. I feel afraid.

She places her hand on Maritza's shoulder.

"That is all right, Maritza. I understand you had no choice."

I can't understand why they are both so frightened. I am excited to meet *real* soldiers, *officers* no less. My tin soldiers are boring now that I have real soldiers in our house.

We step over the threshold. Mutika takes off her backpack and goes to Maritza's small bathroom in the back of the apartment to wash. She comes out wearing lipstick and eye shadow, her wavy auburn hair free of the bandana.

Maritza leads us into the living room where the two men sit around the table and drink coffee. They stand up and click their heels bowing at their waist. I stare at them and raise my hand to my forehead in a crisp salute. I am impressed by their grey uniforms, the lines of medals on their chests, silver swastikas on their collars, and riding trousers tucked into their shiny black boots.

The two of them, stand next to each other. They look so odd. One is fat and short, while the other is tall and skinny. They remind me of Stan Laurel and Oliver Hardy. Their revolvers in black leather holsters and belts are curled like snakes in the middle of the table.

"Guten Morgen gnedige Frau!" They speak almost in unison.

"Guten Morgen!" Mutika responds in German.

"Ich bin Hauptmann Otto Gruber," the fat one says.

"Und, Ich bin Leutnant Josef Kunstler," announces the tall one.

"Pleased to meet you, Hauptmann Gruber and Leutnant Kunstler. I am Piroska Peći and this is my son, Lubo."

"Oh, Madam, please, let's not stand on formalities. Just call me Otto and my comrade Josef. Both Josef and I are from a small village, Schwabing next to Munich. We are simple family men on our way to the Greek front. We will be gone in a few days. We deeply apologize for the intrusion and would be happy to sleep in the den, and now that you are back let you use your bedroom."

"No, no, that is not necessary." Mutika says calmly. "You are already in the bedroom. I insist you stay there. My son and I will sleep in the den."

Hauptman Otto squats down, his face smelling of after shave next to mine, and asks me if I speak German as well, "Schprichst du auch Deutsch?"

"Ya, natürlich." I respond, proud that I can speak to the officer and happy that he pays special attention to me.

"How old are you?" he asks.

"I will be seven in August."

His green eyes sparkle as he smiles and says, "I have a son your age. You look so much like him." I notice his big hands as he reaches for a thick wallet in his back pocket and pulls out a crinkled photograph of a small boy, wearing short leather pants like the ones I have; he is standing next to an older lady in a plain black dress.

"This is Hans and my wife Trudi."

"Where are they?" I ask.

"I have not seen them for quite some time. They are in Schwabing. I miss them so much." He gives me a hug, and I feel his big belly against my body.

"Can Hans and I be good friends and play together?"

Otto says, "Yes, I know Hans would like you."

I don't like Lieutenant Josef. From his stern stare at Otto, I sense that he disapproves that his commanding officer is friendly and talking to me. Mutika's stare reflects her disapproval and she seems not comfortable as well; but does not say anything. Otto is my friend. They are just jealous.

I notice two large rifles in the corner of the room, and rummage through my toy chest for my toy rifle.

"I have a gun as well," I declare and point my toy gun at them. They both smile.

"Would you like to hold a *real* gun?" Hauptman Otto asks me as he pulls out one of the handguns from the black holster and takes out the bullet magazine. I eagerly nod, my eyes fixated on the metal gun, "Yes!"

"This is a German Luger." He hands me the pistol. I smell the strange mixture of oil, polished steel, and a faint odor of gunpowder, as I grasp the wooden grip with two hands.

"Wow! It is heavy." I exclaim. My hands sag and I almost drop the Luger on the floor.

"Before you handle a real Luger you need to grow up some more. Here, maybe if you wear a hat you will look more like a soldier." He picks up his officers hat with the black shiny visor and puts it on my head. My small head sinks into the hat covering up my eyes and ears. I raise my hand to the rim of the hat and give them a crisp salute.

They burst out in a roar of laughter.

I hate being small. I wish I were grown up like them. I can't wait. I would love to wear a uniform and shiny black boots like theirs.

That night in bed, I can't fall asleep. I imagine playing with Hans. Both of us are wearing smart uniforms tucked into our shiny boots. We have small Lugers, tucked into holsters on belts around our waists and perfectly fitting hats on our heads.

We stand at attention next to each other as Hauptman Otto inspects the medals and the shiny swastikas on our uniforms.

The next day at breakfast, Hauptman Otto surprises us. "We received our orders to leave this evening."

I am crushed. Where are they going? It was so much fun spending time with real soldiers rather than playing with my tin soldier army.

"When will you come back?" I ask.

"I don't know. We hope real soon," Otto says, a sad expression on his face.

That evening as they depart our house Hauptman Otto tells Mutika.

"I want to thank you for your hospitality, and wish you the best."

After they are gone Mutika sighs with relief. "I am so glad that these bastard hypocrites have left. Last week they bombed Belgrade and tried to kill us and now they are nice and wish us well. Good riddance!"

I don't know what 'bastard hypocrites' means, but I know I will miss my new friend Hauptman Otto.

Ž

I am sad when the German soldiers leave, but everyone is preoccupied in the house. I seem to get in everyone's way. Mutika is deep in thought and distant. She endlessly rummages through the drawers, looking for something. When I ask her what is the matter she just answers, "Don't worry, my love." But I do worry. Things are just not right. Kolega is still away in the military. I miss him. I wish he were here. The tin soldiers are my only friends. I rearrange them and lead them to war, into battles I copy from the news I hear on the radio; as of German troops invade Poland, Austria, and Czechoslovakia.

Kolega finally comes home. I am so happy to see him again. I run to him and hug him. I feel the rough material of his grey military uniform. When he takes off his Šajkača, a cap that looks like a small upturned boat, I see his closely cropped head and start laughing. I point my finger at him.

"You look really funny. What happened to your hair?"

"They shaved my head in the army," he tells me, and proceeds to take off his uniform.

"Don't take your uniform off," I insist. "I like it. When you were gone the German officers who stayed with us, kept their uniforms on."

I am all excited as I tell him about our guests, the insignia on their uniforms, and the guns they let me hold, but his look tells me he is not pleased.

"Where did you park the car?" Mutika asks Kolega.

"I drove it off a cliff."

"Did you get into an accident?" Mutika has a worried look on her face.

"No. No. Don't worry," he says. "The Germans ordered all Jews to turn their cars in. I would be darned if I were going to give them my car. I drove it up the mountain, put it in gear, and let it roll off a cliff. I will tell them it was an accident."

I am sad. I loved riding in that car. If Kolega's car had an extra wheel in front, like my 'SCHUCO' toy car, it would have not fallen off the cliff.

With Kolega's return, I was hoping that everything would be normal again. But no, everyone remains worried. Mutika and Kolega, their faces stern, keep whispering to each other about something. Occasionally they raise their voices and I hear "We can't do this." or "We should do that."

"What is going on?" I wonder.

The rest of the week gets worse with each passing day. I catch snippets of conversation, not really understanding and too afraid to ask questions. Mutika is saying something about a new law and how she has to give to the government her beautiful gold bracelet. The bracelet must weigh enough to meet what each Jewish family must give to the government. I don't understand. *What will the government do with Mutika's bracelet? Who is going to wear it?* The only gold I ever had was the 'Hanukah Gelt', chocolate coins covered in gold foil. If I didn't eat them already, maybe my coins would be enough, and Mutika could keep her bracelet.

A few days later, Kolega brings home two yellow freshly minted round aluminum badges. There is a big black Ž printed in the middle. Every Jew must wear one on the lapel when they go out into the street.

"Where is my badge? How come I did not get one?"

"You don't have to wear one. Children don't need to wear a badge," Kolega tells me.

Everyone always tells me that I am a big boy and besides, I am also a Jew. It is not fair; I want to wear the same badge. I get my crayons, make a crude yellow paper sign, with a backward Ž, and pin it on my lapel. Kolega gets very angry and rips it off, telling me:

"I told you before, only adults must wear the sign." I burst into tears.

The next day there is a knock at our door and a man hands Kolega a piece of paper that says that he has to report to the police. I am frightened. They will arrest him for destroying his car.

"Don't go," I beg him.

He calms me. "Don't worry, all Jewish men have to report to the police and register. It is just a formality. I will be back in no time."

When he doesn't return that evening Mutika dresses and tells me, "I am going to see a German business friend of Kolega. I should be back very soon. You mind Maritza while I am gone."

Now with both gone, I am left alone with Maritza and my tin soldiers. The maid puts me to bed. I toss and turn. Sleep does not come easily.

I wake up the next morning. Both my parents are back and busy packing several suitcases.

"Where are we going?" I ask.

"We are going to your Grandma's house. Hurry up and get dressed."

"Why do we have to leave in such a hurry?" I ask.

"If we don't leave right away the police will arrest Kolega again. Grandma lives on the other side of town. They will not look there."

I think to myself: "This is so exciting. Like in the movies, we are running away from the police. I am happy, Kolega and Mutika are back and that we are going to my Grandma's."

I love going to Grandma's house. Heated by the fire in the wood stove, her place is always warm and cozy. The house smells of baking pastry, freshly brewed coffee, boiling cabbage, meat sauces, laundry bleach, and grilled onions. She always puts her brown freckled hand on my cheek and greets me with "Lubo! *Edesh gyermek*!" That means: 'Sweet Child', in her strange Hungarian language.

We take a taxi to Grandma's house, and after we put the luggage in the spare bedroom, we all sit in the kitchen.

Mutika tells everyone what happened last night.

"When Kolega reported to the police, they arrested him and took him with many of our Jewish male friends to a large warehouse in the Exposition Park outside Zagreb. After he did not come home that evening, I decided to see his German business client and ask what he could do to help me. Could he write a note, and request that they release Kolega from jail, so that he can assist him to get an urgent shipment through customs? Only after he seriously warned me was he was kind enough to write the note.

'This is the only note I will ever write for you. I am doing this because both you and your husband are my good friends. What I am doing is very dangerous for me. After today, I will deny that I ever knew you. You might not realize, but you are in grave danger. You and your husband must disappear. Go as far as you can from here. Find a safe place. If they catch you they will kill you.'

After profusely thanking him," Mutika continued, "I took the note to the police and they released Kolega on a twenty-four hour pass. We could not think of where to go so we came here."

For the next week we stay at my grandmother's house, too afraid to go out in the street. Strict laws prohibit Jews to travel and leave town. Mutika finds out that some of our friends already left for Italy, after they converted to the Catholic religion. They are safe in Treviso, a small town outside Venice.

I don't really understand what Catholic means and why only they are allowed to travel. The next day we all go to the church. I have never been in a church. It is beautiful. Light shines through the stained glass windows, each one showing a different picture and casting a colorful pattern on the floor. On a raised platform, in front of the row of pews, is a table covered by a white embroidered tablecloth. In the middle of the table sits a big silver cross, flanked by several candlesticks. Above the altar is a naked man wearing a diaper, nailed by his hands and feet to a huge wooden cross. Blood is dripping from his hands, feet, and the big wound in his chest. How scary.

A priest in a long white skirt and a lace collar greets us. We kneel in the pew of the first row. He mumbles something in a language I do not understand, waving his hands above our heads. He daubs his finger in a bowl of water and wets my forehead. Then he gets a bowl, and scoops a small amount of sugar with a small silver spoon. He offers it to first to Kolega, who swallows a small amount, then to Mutika, and finally at last to me. I eagerly take the whole amount and immediately start to choke. It is not sugar! It is salt. He tricked me.

We go into the side office, and the priest writes something on a large sheet of parchment with a picture of the church. He licks several colorful stamps and sticks them on the parchment. He takes a round rubber stamp and with two loud thumps marks the stamps on the parchment. He congratulates us and declares that now we are Catholics. I don't feel any different, beside the bitter salty taste in my mouth.

The next day my parents sit me down and tell me, "It is too dangerous for us to stay here. We have to run away to Italy. It will be too risky for you to come with us. We might have to walk at night over the mountains. You will be much safer with Aunt Babuš, and Uncle Štefko in Brod until we can bring you to Italy. They are Catholic and you will be much safer with them."

Then both my mother and father insist, "You must never tell anybody that you are Jewish."

I don't understand any of this. The only thing I hear is that my parents are leaving me.

"I don't want to go to Aunt Babuš. I want to go with you." I protest through my tears.

Kolega and Mutika try to calm me:

"Once we are settled we will send for you."

"Promise? Word of honor?"

"Yes. Of course," they reply. But, I don't believe them.

My parents get ready for the trip. Between a large purse and a small suitcase, they must be able to carry everything they wish to take. Mutika sells all our possessions and changes the money into gold coins, jewelry and dollar bills. She buys an expensive fur coat, which can be sold for cash, if needed. She sews the dollar bills into the linings of the coat, the skirt, and Kolega's pants. I watch Kolega as he hides the gold coins in the heels of the shoes. He peels the first layer of leather from the heel and with a sharp knife carves out the other layer centers making a hollow space in the heel to hold the coins. To keep them from jiggling and making noise as one walks, Kolega cuts up several candles, melts them on the stove in a small pan and pours the molten wax over the coins in the cavity. Finally he hammers the first layer back on the heel. The shoe, although very heavy, looks just like a regular shoe.

In the evening, before going to bed, I try again to convince them to take me with them.

"Please, don't leave me. I want to go with you. I will be so good."

They hug me, tears in their eyes, as they try to calm me again. They repeat their promise that I will rejoin them as soon as they settle in Italy. That night as I lay in bed, I keep hoping they will change their minds the next morning and take me with them.

I wake up the next morning and look for them. I can't find them. They left while I was still asleep.

*   *   *

Years later Mutika told me that they left early that day to avoid detection.

They took a train to the border city of Rijeka, separated by a bridge over the river from Fiume, on the Italian side. They did not know what awaited them. At the border crossing, the train stopped and several tall, good-looking *Carabinieri*, the Italian police, came to check the documents. They spoke only Italian and Mutika would have given anything to be able to speak with them. They kept repeating *"Bukuritza, Bukuritza"* but Mutika did not understand what that meant. *"Bukuritza"* is "Bakar", site of the Italian internment camp for refugees. The Carabinieri tried to send my parents there.

"Treviso, Treviso" my parents repeated.

Finally through gestures and pointing of fingers, it became clear that my parents could either go to where the Carabinieri indicated, or get off the train. Kolega and Mutika chose to get off the train in Rijeka. Mutika put on her heavy fur coat; they picked up their small suitcases, got off the train, and walked, in the July heat, to the waterfront near by.

After talking to the local fishermen, Mutika found out that for a fee equal to almost a week's wages, one of them was willing to take them out in his rowboat and let them off on the Italian side. They boarded the small rowboat and the fisherman started rowing straight out. The beach, on that summer day, was full of bathers on colorful towels spread on the sand, and children splashing in the water. Mutika in her heavy fur coat recalled that she was shivering in fear. The fisherman rowed out to sea, until the rowboat appeared as just a speck from the shore, and no one on the beach noticed when he started rowing towards the Italian side. After a while he rowed the boat back to land in Italy.

Just like the Croat beach, the shore on the other side was full of bathers. Mutika and Kolega came ashore and stepped on to the wet sand in their heavy gold-filled shoes. People on the beach stared at them, obviously puzzled by the sight of a man in a heavy overcoat accompanied by a lady wearing a fur coat as they marched on the hot sand. They must be out of their minds. Ignoring the stares, Kolega and Mutika trudged toward the street. They reached the Fiume railroad station and within several hours boarded the train to Treviso, where they knew they would find shelter with our friends already there.

Arrival in Brod

A few days after my parents left, Aunt Babuš comes to Zagreb. She helps me pack my clothes. I insist on taking my tin soldiers and my toy rifle that barely fits sideways into my tiny suitcase. That afternoon we board the train at the main station in Zagreb and arrive the same evening in Brod. Uncle Štefko and my twin cousins Hanzi and Greta, meet us at the station. After many warm embraces Uncle Štefko, hails a "Fijaker", a black horse drawn carriage. The first Fijaker, from a row of several similar ones lined across the street, starts to move. The drumbeat of horse hooves against the cobblestones is accompanied by the squeak of two small carriage wheels in front and two large ones in back. The coachman in a thick leather jacket sits on the high perch in front; his legs covered by a thick blanket, a heavy scarf wrapped around his neck, and a black fedora on his head as he holds the reins with his left hand and wields a long whip in his right.

He jumps off the carriage and loads my small suitcase below the folding canvas top in the back.

I would love to sit on that high perch, so I ask Uncle Štefko "Can I sit up there with the man?"

"Let me ask him."

"Do you know how to drive the horses?" the coachman asks.

I nod my head with excitement. "Yes. I have a horse, but I could not take him on the train and had to leave him in Zagreb."

"All right, then." The coachman smiles and lifts me up.

Uncle Štefko, Babuš, Hanzi, and Greta, sit in the Fijaker's cushioned seats. The coachman climbs next to me, grabs the reins, snaps his whip with a loud crack and the two horses begin to pull the coach. I watch their shiny big round brown rumps shift with each step, muscles straining to pull the load, their black tails swinging from side to side. I can only see the black mane and their ears and blinders sticking out from their heads.

"My horse's name is Malen. What are the names of your two horses?"

"The one on the left is called 'Leva' and the one on the right is called 'Desna'," he says, a big grin on his face, as he winks at me.

I wonder why would anyone name his horses 'Left' and 'Right'?

"OK. Let's see if you can really drive the carriage." He hands me the reins and the whip.

I stiffen feeling scared, almost petrified. The horses continue their leisurely pace and I slowly relax, so proud to drive the horse-carriage and feel like a grown up man.

We reach a church square surrounded by tall mulberry trees and turn to a dirt road with whitewashed single story houses on one side, and a long brown wooden fence on the other. We stop in front of a house with a large wooden gate on one side.

"Here we are," says Uncle Štefko. He helps

me down from my high perch, unloads my suitcase, and pays the driver. I wave at the coachman as the Fijaker pulls away. Aunt Babuš opens a small door in the gate and we enter a courtyard.

"This is your new home," she says, pointing to the house on the left.

I don't want a new home. I want to go back to Zagreb. I want my mother and father.

We enter the house and Aunt Babuš leads me to a small room. "Here is the room you will share with Hanzi and Greta and there is your bed."

She points to a small cot under a large window that overlooks the courtyard.

"Here is Greta's bed and this is Hanzi's bed." And points to two large beds on each side of the wall.

I miss my parents, and do not want to be here, but I am happy to sleep in the same room with my fourteen-year-old cousins.

After supper I go to bed and lay awake, unable to sleep, thinking about all that happened in the last few weeks. I wish I could be with my family in our Zagreb apartment.

The next morning Hanzi wakes me up.

"Picane," he calls, using my new nickname, which means little squirt. "Put on your bathing suit. We are going swimming in the river today."

I run and put on my bathing suit. I remember our vacation In Juan Les Pins and how I enjoyed wading and splashing in the sea.

We walk down a dirt road to the river Sava, descend the bank and follow the fast running water until we reach a bend where the current slows down and forms a still swimming hole. Hanzi runs through the shallow water into the deep, dives, and disappears under the surface. I cautiously follow, my feet sinking into the mud with each step, until the water reaches my waist. I don't know how to swim and splash in the shallow part. Hanzi head pops up near me and says:

"Come on. Swim to me."

"I don't know how to swim." I protest.

"Oh! Well I will teach you." He holds me on top of the water with my arms extended in front of me. "Kick your feet and push back with your arms."

That summer we go swimming almost every day and by the end of the summer Hanzi and I swim together in the deeper water. Greta does not come swimming with us. She is a girl.

She usually stays home to cook dinner. At times I stay home and help her. She teaches me how to peel potatoes, how long to boil them and then mash them and mix them with butter and milk. Greta shows me how to dip the chicken thighs, legs, and wings first in flour, then beaten eggs, and finally in breadcrumbs, before she places them in the pan with hot bubbly fat. I love mashed potatoes and fried chicken.

Greta has long black hair, just like Aunt Babuš. She wears it in two long braids that swing over her shoulders. Aunt Babuš has one braid that she coils in a bun and pins to the back of her head. After Greta washes her hair she combs it into two long bulky strands on each side of her head. She divides each one further into three thinner ones and braids them into a long braid tying the end with a rubber band. She teaches me how to do it. I love combing and braiding her long hair.

Greta was born ten minutes before Hanzi, but Hanzi claims that he is older because he is a male. They fight over this all the time and sometimes they chase each other all over the house.

"You have to listen to me. I am older than you. I was born ten minutes before you." Greta says this to Hanzi when he does not want to take the trash out.

"No you are not. I am a boy, and males are always older."

He starts to walk away, but Greta has a quick temper and picks up a seltzer bottle and squirts a steady stream at the back of Hanzi's head. He turns around and starts running after Greta. She runs into the next room and locks the door.

"You are not only younger than me, you are chicken as well." He yells through the locked door. He turns to me, grabs me by my hand and exclaims, "Girls! Come, lets get out of here."

I follow Hanzi everywhere he and his friends go. Hanzi and his friends accept me as a member of their secret society "The Black Spider". We climb a spiral staircase to the top of the church tower and sit in a circle in the round tower attic. Hanzi gets his penknife out and after wiping it on his trousers, takes my index finger and pricks it with the tip of the blade. I can't cry in front of all the boys and just blurt a quiet "Ouch." A small drop of blood forms on the tip of my finger.

Hanzi repeats the ritual, pricking everyone's finger. We join our bloody fingers together as we all repeat in chorus after him, "With my blood - I swear allegiance - to the 'The Black Spider' secret society. Under penalty - of death - I will never reveal - any of our secrets."

"Congratulations. You are now a Black Spider," announces Hanzi. I am so proud. I am a big boy.

The group immediately puts me to work. We decide to steal some food from the rectory basement next to the church. I, being the smallest, wiggle through the small window into the parish larder. I land on the hard floor. It is dark. My eyes take a while to adjust. I stare, amazed. Hams, bacon, sausages, and various smoked meat hang on steel wires between two walls. Bottles of wine in dark flasks, one on top of each other, line the wooden shelves along the walls. I try to reach one of the hams, but it is too high. I jump, grab hold of it, lift my feet, and put my whole weight on it. I hear a loud crack. The steel wire snaps. I still am holding tight to the ham as I tumble down followed by the rest of the meat. I lay there, scared to move, scared that the door will open any minute and a priest will appear.

All is quiet, except the loud pounding of my heart. I finally get up and start to hand Hanzi the ham, a few strands of sausages, and several bottles of wine. I try to get out through the window, but it is too high. I panic, but luckily I spot an empty crate, move it to the window and scramble out.

We run to the church and climb the steps, two at a time, to our lair in the tower attic. Hanzi slices the meat, giving each one a piece. He uncorks a bottle with the corkscrew of his Swiss Army knife. We pass the bottle around. Everyone takes a swig. I love the ham and the sausages, but, after taking a small sip, I find that I don't like wine. Every time my turn comes, no one notices that I don't swallow and only pretend to drink.

I make friends with the neighborhood kids. We climb up the mulberry trees by the church, sit on the branches, munch on the purple fruit, and throw the ripe berries at each other. In the evening I return home with thick purple lips and berry blotches all over my body. I am shirtless and wear only my bathing suit.

On other days we run in the dust clouds left by the passing cars on the street in front of our house. We soon tire of running behind the cars and dare each other to cross the street and run just in front of the cars. I run in front of one of the cars. The car stops. The driver gets out of the car. He runs after me. He catches me, grabs me by my hand, and proceeds to spank me on my rear as he yells, "What is the matter with you crazy kids? Do you want to get killed?"

I wet my pants, the flow down my leg mixes with the dust into muddy spots. The man lets me go and I, ashamed to show my muddy legs to my friends, run to the river to wash off my shame. After that we stop running behind and in front of the cars.

Hanzi and Greta adopt me as their little brother. That summer I hardly think about my parents.

The time passes quickly, and one day Aunt Babuš says "Now that fall is approaching, you are ready to start school." I really don't want to go to school. I want to stay home and play with my friends.

The next day Aunt Babuš gives me a bath and brushes my hair. She puts on my fine clothing that feel so strange after wearing just a bathing suit all summer.

The schoolhouse, in a two story grey building with a wide staircase leading to the entrance, is only a few blocks away from our house. Aunt Babuš comes with me and enrolls me in the office on the first floor. As she leaves, I don't hug her goodbye. I am a big boy now and too embarrassed to hug her in front of the other children. I climb upstairs and enter my assigned room 2B. A large blackboard and a crucifix hang on the wall in front of children sitting in rows of small school desks. The teacher is a nun like the kind I used to see near the cathedral in Zagreb. This one looks stern in her black habit and bright white starched wimple as she points to an empty seat.

"You can sit there," she announces.

"We start our class with a prayer. Since Jews are not allowed to say the Lord's Prayer, all Jewish children need to stand against that wall." She points with her finger to the wall.

Several boys and girls get up and line with

their backs against the wall.

I feel as one of them and want to join them, but remember that I am not allowed to let anyone know I am Jewish. I sit tightly in my seat. From the corner of my eyes I watch the sad faces, yearning to be the same as the rest of the children and not outcasts, not rejects, not defective.

Can they read my mind and tell that I am Jewish? I fear one of them will say "He is Jewish. He should stand with us against the wall?"

In fear or shame, I avert my eyes. We all bow our heads, our hands clasped, and the nun leads us in prayer. I bury my head in my hands as I mouth sounds, pretending to know the words of the prayer.

School lasts only half a day. I already know how to read and finish my homework quickly. This leaves me with lots of free time.

I spend many afternoons in Uncle Štefko's warm tailor shop on the main square. He and his two assistants sit cross-legged on top of wooden tables, sewing with wide strokes by hand. They baste the cloth with white thread and then sew it together on the foot pedal sewing machines. Once they are finished, it is my job to pull the basting out. I like my job. I love doing grown up work.

In preparation for my First Communion each Wednesday after supper I go to my Catechism classes. I learn that before I can get my communion, I have to go to confession where I will have to list all my sins. Our Catechisms teacher tells us that it is a sin to steal, lie, or cheat.

"Do I also have to confess that I lied about being Jewish?" I ask Greta, who assures me

"No. This is not a sin. Never, never, tell any one that you are Jewish." I feel much better.

Next Sunday in church, we line up in front of the confessional and wait our turn. I am preoccupied with counting the number of times I lied, cheated, or stole. My turn comes up very quickly and I kneel in front of the little window. I can see the head of the priest through the small grating.

I quickly cross myself and blurt the words we were taught in our Catechism classes:

"In the name of the Father, and of the Son, and of the Holy Spirit. Bless me father for I have sinned." I quickly continue in a trembling voice — I want to get it over with.

"I lied four times, cheated three, and stole two times." I can see the priest smile and assume my ordeal is over, until he asks me, "And, did you play with that thing in your pants?"

I panic. I don't understand. What thing in my pants? What am I supposed to do with that thing in my pants? What does he mean?

"No." I fearfully stammer, shaking my head furiously.

He frowns and gives me a penance of three Hail Mary's and absolves my sins. Other boys get many more. I was very lucky.

After church I tell Hanzi about what happened and ask him "What are you supposed to do with that thing in your pants?"

"I will show you." He unzips his pants as if to pee, but starts to stroke his 'Pisher' that grows like Pinocchio's nose and suddenly squirts a few drops of white snot on the ground. I try to do the same, but mine remains shrunken and small. I can only pee with my little pisher. I am relieved that I am unable to sin.

The following Sunday, I put on my best clothes, and go to mass to receive my First Communion. My Catechism teacher explained that the wafer the priest places on our tongues represents the body of Jesus Christ and the wine His blood. We should not chew the wafer, and just to let it melt on our palate. We are supposed to take only a very small sip of the wine. I remember a scary movie "Fräulein" took me to in Zagreb. In the movie the natives in Africa boil the explorers in big iron vats. Is this how they make the wafers? And how do they make wine from blood? It just does not make sense!

We kneel in the first row, boys in their best clothing, girls in white wedding dresses with white gauze veils trimmed with flowers, eyes closed, mouths open wide, like hungry birds, their tongues stuck out. The priest goes from child to child. He picks a white round wafer from a chalice, waives it in the sign of the cross, and places it in each gaping mouth. My wafer sticks to my palate and I barely suppress the cough welling in my throat. I think, at least it does not taste like the salt the priest gave me in Zagreb.

Lou Pechi

<u>Diamond Ring</u>

It finally stopped snowing in the morning.

The fresh white snow sparkles in the bright sun's rays. It is a crisp and brilliant December day. The spring piglet bought last year, now a big porker, has grown so much he is barely able to move in the pigsty in back of the house.

When we first got the cute little piglet I told Uncle Štefko "He is so cute. What should we name him?"

"Oh, we never name our pig," my uncle replied. "It is just too hard to slaughter one with a name."

I am so glad I have a name.

I think that maybe if I give him a name he won't be slaughtered. I decide to name him "Pig". That way nobody will realize he has a real name.

Pig snorts and emits puffs of steam that rise into the sky. I approach the sty. Accustomed to his morning feeding, he presses his snout through the gaps in the boards; happy someone is going to feed him.

"Sorry," I tell him. "Today there is no breakfast. This is your big day. Today is slaughter day. I came to say goodbye to you."

He grunts, and I scratch his head.

"I will miss you so much."

I will miss bringing his daily bucket of slop; potato peels, spoiled vegetables, remnants of our meals, all mixed with old milk and water. Pig gives me a few understanding snorts, moves away in the sty, only to return, and poke his snout again through the well-worn cracks for another pat on the head.

I linger around the pigsty, trying to spend as much time with Pig as possible. He never harmed anyone. Why do we have to take his life? My thoughts are interrupted by a noise from the gate.

Four men carry strange utensils on their shoulders as they file through the entrance. They wear big white aprons tied by a string around their fat necks. White wisps of steam rise from their mouths. Their stocky bodies fill their tight clothes, almost as if someone blew them up like balloons. Their puffed cheeks radiate with glow of rich food and hard work. They remind me of Pig, his pink skin stretched over his fat body that filled up over they summer, and is ready to burst.

Three of them are young and seem to follow the orders of the older fourth one. He is the head butcher, the crew chief.

"You", he says, as he points to the man wearing a cap, "Start the water boiling."

The young man lifts a big pot, places it on a metal stand, pours several buckets of water into it, lights a fire underneath, and in no time, a plume of grey smoke, and a flickering fire rises from the bottom.

Amidst joking and cheering comments the men unload an assortment of knives, sausage presses, hoists, and a huge polished wooden tub, seemingly carved from a single piece of wood. They move, like well-synchronized circus clowns, among the haphazardly strewn equipment. Their black rubber boots slap their calves, creating an echo with each step they take. They spot me watching them on the side.

"Hey Picane, what is your name?" the boss shouts.

"Lubo."

Their direct and sudden approach does not even give me time to feel frightened or embarrassed. He asks me, "Lubo, how would you like to be a butcher's assistant for today?"

I eagerly nod.

"Good. Today we have a very important job for you. See that washbasin there. Go and fetch it." I run and bring him the basin.

"Good. Now listen very carefully. You are to be next to me at all the times. Don't let me out of your sight. When we catch the pig you are to be right there to make sure and collect all the blood in the basin."

He laughs and winks at the other three. "If any blood spills on the ground you will have to lick it clean, so make sure to catch every single drop in the basin."

I stare, frozen stiff with the thought of licking the whole yard clean.

He takes a large knife and a stone sharpener from the pile of tools on the wooden table, holds the wooden knife handle in one hand, and slides it's worn out blade across the sharpener held in his other. He reminds me of Toma, the barber I hated in

Zagreb, who sharpened his razor by sliding it across a leather strap.

He slips the knife into a leather sheath tied to a belt wrapped around his fat belly.

"All right, open the door." He yells at one of the men standing near the pigsty. Bedlam breaks out.

Pig, sensing the first freedom in his life, dashes out of the sty. He runs toward the farthest corner of the yard. There is no exit. He turns quickly. He dashes in the other direction. The men follow him with their clumsy waddling run from one end of the yard to the other. Pig is fast, but they are many. I try to tag along.

I think to myself, "Why did they let 'Pig' out when they could easily catch him in the confined space of the pigsty? Why did they let him loose and make me run all over the yard? I hope he escapes."

But I don't have time to ponder my questions as I scurry after the head butcher. My heart pounds from running in circles. My prayers are not answered. Suddenly the young butcher in the cap, grabs the two rear trotters of Pig, twists them, loses his cap, and Pig rolls on his back in the middle of the yard.

The other men grab the front trotters and Pig squeals in a high-pitched voice I never heard before. The sound drowns the yells of the butchers. Pig knows this is his end and tries in vain to call for help. Tears well in my eyes, as I seem to be the only one who understands Pig. Yet I can't help. I can't change the injustice being done to him.

The head butcher, draws a large knife from its sheath and slides the long blade in a slow and deliberate motion into the fat under the Pig's throat. I can hear the loud beat of my heart, while there is no sound from the knife as it slips back out followed by the red gushing stream of red blood. A steamy, rusty, salty, metallic smell fills my lungs as I bend over, eyes focused on the pulsating stream trying to catch every spurt, without spilling a drop. "Boom. Boom. Boom." Beats the Pig's heart, as each beat spews another gush of the red liquid into the basin. Slow down, I pray, the washbasin is getting full. Slow down, please. Just in time the beats slow down and become smaller and smaller. Pig gives a last jerk, as his blubbery body, still tightly grasped by the butchers, sinks to the ground.

"Good bye Pig." I mumble to myself. One of the men takes the basin away, and praises me on a job well done. The dead body is no longer my Pig; it is just a pig.

Two men lift the pot from the fire and pour the boiling water into the wooden tub. White steam clouds rise into the air. Then, each man grabs a trotter, as they gently lift the pig and lay him on his back in the tub.

Four limbs point up into heaven. Excess water spills over the rim. They start to shave his few black hairs with their sharp knives, down to his skin's pink nakedness. The men grunt, pick the body out of the tub, and hang it by the hind legs on the wooden braces. The pig swings as if on gallows, his nose almost touching the ground. The leader takes out the same knife and in his rugged graceful motions proceeds to unzip the belly of the pig with the sharp tip. Steam rises out of the still warm pig's body. Blue and greenish tinged guts and entrails roll into the pail underneath. I stand motionless, mouth wide open, too scared to scream and too fascinated to run away. With deft motions the butcher cuts around the cavity, carving around the bones, knowing every soft spot of the animal, until the pig is split in half. The fat skin is next, as he proceeds to cut it into thick squares of white raw bacon that he tosses in to a waiting pot. As soon as the pot is full two men lift it and place it on the fire to render the fat.

Another butcher picks up the pail with the entrails and begins to squeeze them. Hot foul stench, similar to the one in the pig's sty, emanates from the green grey ooze plopping into another pail. He throws the squeezed guts into the wooden tub and washes them, rubbing one against the other, same as our laundress does with our laundry. I approach cautiously staring at the pail of guts. The other men stop their work and slowly congregate around me.

"Lubo, guess what we found in the pig's belly?" the foreman says.

I just shrug my shoulders.

"We found a diamond ring," he says as he winks to his companions. "Since you did such a good job we decided that you should have it."

"Really? You mean it?" My eyes widen with excitement.

"Yes. Just stick you finger out and I will place it on your finger."

I extend my right index finger. He slips something round and slippery on it. The men erupt in a roar of laughter. At first I don't understand what they are laughing about. I look at my finger and see that the round thing on my finger is not a diamond ring. I really don't know that the slippery piece is the pig's rectum, cut to resemble a ring. I pull the slimy thing off in disgust, toss it on the ground, and run to the house to wash my hands and hide my shame. The laughter follows me into the bathroom where I stay until my sobs subside.

"They tricked me," I tell myself. "But, I will not let them get away with it."

I grit my teeth and utter proudly "Za inat" — a Serbian word of stubbornness and defiance I learned from Hanzi. It means to do something regardless of consequences. I wipe my tears and return to the courtyard to face my tormentors. "I will show them," I mumble under my breath.

Arrest

Dinner is almost over and I am sopping the chicken juices on my plate with a piece of fresh white bread. I have been living in Brod for almost two years when the doorbell starts to ring followed by loud knocks on the house gate.

Uncle Štefko goes to the door and I hear him say, "Who is it?" Curious, I get off my chair to see who it is.

I hear a loud brusque voice.

"Police. Open the door".

Uncle Štefko opens the door. I see two tall men in long trench coats, their faces in the shadow of brown fedoras on their heads.

"What can I do for you?" My uncle inquires in a shrill and quivering voice quite different from his normal tone. I realize he is frightened, and his panic gets hold of me.

"We have a warrant for the arrest for Lubo Peći."

"What has he done? He is only eight years old." Uncle Štefko, terror in his voice, tries to argue with the men.

"We don't have that information. We only have our orders to bring him to the police station. You can inquire later with the chief of police."

Uncle Štefko argues with the men to no avail and, in resignation, Aunt Babuš puts on my heavy coat.

"Don't worry. You'll be fine." She tries to

reassure me as I hug her and don't want to let go.

One of the men gets hold of my hand and pulls me away from her. We leave, and I march between the two men toward the police station.

What did I do to be arrested? Did they find out about my stealing from the church rectory? My mind races, as I try to go over the previous few weeks and figure what I did do to cause these men to take me away. *Maybe I should just run away? I can run much faster than these men. Where could I run? Home would not be safe. Perhaps the best is to just behave and not make matters worse.*

We reach the police station and the two men turn me over to another man sitting behind a desk, who writes my name in a big ledger in front of him. They take me to an empty cell with a chair in the middle of the room and tell me to sit. A man in a white coat puts an apron around my neck and begins to shear off my hair leaving me totally bald. I feel like Pig when the butchers shaved him after the slaughter and look bald like Kolega when he came back from the military service.

Another man in a police uniform takes me into a small cell already filled with women and children. Old women, in dark clothes, black headscarves on their gray heads, sit along the walls and clutch scanty quilts to their knees. Several boys and girls, much younger than me, blankets up to their necks sleep on the floor. I am tired, and find an empty space in a corner. I pull my knees to my chin and let the events of the day lull me into sleep.

The next morning I wake up and find a

backpack with some of my belongings next to me; Aunt Babuš has brought it to the police station during the night. Someone announces that there is a parade going on outside. Everyone scurries and crowds the window. I try to elbow my way to the front, but am too short to reach the bars.

"Please let me see the procession. My cousin Greta is marching. I want to see her." I plead desperately.

A woman picks me up and I grasp the iron bars with my two small hands, straining to keep my head above the casement. In front of the procession several big boys carry colorful church flags. Four men follow and carry a platform with 'Mother Mary' in flowing blue robes clutching Infant Jesus. Behind them bleeding, Jesus stretched on a wooden cross, stiffly stares with his blind plaster eyes. I see my cousin Greta, in a white dress, among the marchers. She looks up and spots me in the widow. Our eyes lock. Tears stream down her face. I want to shout, "Greta. I want to be with you in that parade. I want to be with my friends."

I grip the bars in rage. My knuckles turn white. My face contorts in a silent angry scream, "Help!"

But there is no sound. Terrified, afraid, ashamed to be in jail, embarrassed by my shaven head, I cannot utter a sound.

In the meantime, I learn that Aunt Babuš decides to travel to Zagreb the next morning and see if she can somehow obtain a release for me.

Later, she tells me exactly what happened.

Her train from Brod to Zagreb is late as usual. Men with their grey jackets and black hats, pants tucked into their boots, women with flowing skirts and colorful handkerchiefs tied on their heads sit on the ground and on available benches, with baskets of eggs, cheese, and various colorful fruits and produce at their feet. Chickens and geese, tied by their legs, like a bunch of wiggling flowers, chirp and squeak, sensing their impending fate.

Štefko, carries a big basket full of baked goods in one hand, and holds Aunt Babuš by the other. They find a place on a bench and sit quietly, but their worried thoughts carry on a relentless conversation. In Zagreb, Aunt Babuš will try to seek my release from jail. Štefko will stay in Brod.

Aunt Babuš has an impossible task. How is she going to seek a safe passage for a child left behind, when his parents are subject to a warrant for their arrest and have left the country illegally to seek refuge in Italy? Who is she going to contact? Will they listen? Will they help? She must try.

The train arrives. They embrace, their glances full of love for each other. He, wishing her luck in her quest, she hoping to calm his worries.

Aunt Babuš joins the crowd, boards the train, and finds an empty seat in a packed compartment. She does not join the small talk with the other travelers, and is in deep thought about what she can do in Zagreb to save me. She drifts into sleep, only to be awakened by new ideas, new hope, followed by despair soothed again by sleep. The shrill train whistle interrupts her reverie as Zagreb appears in the smoky window.

The next day her host in Zagreb invites her neighbor, Mrs. Milica Müller over for a cup of Turkish coffee. Aunt Babuš tells Mrs. Müller why she is in Zagreb and describes the arrest of her eight-year-old nephew in Brod. Mrs. Müller is horrified. Her son Vlado is almost the same age as I am.

Aunt Babuš asks Mrs. Müller if she has any idea of how to convince Mr. Vinek, the Chief of Police in Brod, to let Lubo out of the jail, before the transport leaves.

"Wait a minute" Mrs. Müller interrupts. " Did you say Vinek? His brother lives here in Zagreb, and is a good friend of mine. Maybe I could talk to him and see if he could intervene with his brother."

A ray of sunshine lights Babuš's face, her eyes widen as the door of hope opens a small crack.

Indeed, after Mrs. Müller talks to Mr. Vinek' brother in Zagreb, he writes a letter to his brother in Brod regarding a wrong done to a family Soldini during the past regime a while ago. His brother in Brod owes him a favor, and releasing the child would clear that favor.

Aunt Babuš immediately leaves Zagreb the next day to personally deliver the letter to the Chief of Police.

Uncle Štefko, who stayed in Brod during that time, begins to write a letter to Mutika in Italy:

5/17/1943

Dear Pišta and Pirika,

Don't be surprised that we are sending this letter instead of Pican whom you expected. From the contents of this letter you will understand what the reason is, and that the most important fact is that he is with us.

By listing all the particulars, I hope I can describe vividly what has happened so that you can have a clear picture and judge for yourself the seriousness of the situation.

On May 4th, 1943, police authorities arrested Lubo and the last of all the Jews in Brod. Babuš went with him to the jail, not wanting to leave him alone among strangers and without anyone from his own family. We quickly found out that the detainees would remain in Brod only two days and then immediately be shipped to Zagreb, and after that, to Germany. I cannot describe our confusion, worry, and the heaviness of this situation. We simply could not relax. I knocked on many doors, crossed many thresholds to no avail.

After a few hours Babuš decided to

leave Lubo alone at the jail. She felt she could be more effective by working for his freedom outside the confines of the prison. So she, working from one side, and I, from the other side, both looked frantically for a way out.

At first, without any success!..........

Meanwhile, in the jail, rumors go around that by midnight the convoy to Germany will be leaving. The tiny cell is by now full of those taken in the last roundup of Jews in Brod. Old women and children sprawl on multicolored blankets, meager belongings neatly stashed at the heads of the makeshift beds, trying to rest. I don't know the other children and pass the time with my tin soldiers. I line the soldiers in a neat row against the wall and shoot at them with the marbles Greta brought me. One by one they topple down.

An old woman, who seems to have adopted me, claims she knows my family, but to me she is a total stranger. She neatly arranges my clothes in the tiny knapsack that my Aunt Babuš brought me. By now she taught me how to fold my blanket in a tight roll and tie it over my knapsack.

Somehow, I am not ready to depart, but eager to leave the confines of the narrow cell, and breathe the fresh outside air.

The heavy steel door of the cell opens and a guard in a gruff voice calls my name.

I am thinking, "What did I do now? Why are they picking me?"

The old lady helps me fold the blanket and neatly tuck it over the backpack as the guard shouts "Hurry up."

I follow the guard through the long hallway and into an empty cell with just a small stool in the middle. The guard tells me to sit on the stool and wait. He shuts the iron door with a thud. Thoughts race through my head faster than I can think. *What are they going to do to me now? They took me from my home the other day, shaved my head, and stuck me in a crowded cell. What is next?*

The opening of the door interrupts my thoughts. A big man in a uniform, an insignia on his shoulders, enters. In a deep loud voice he looks at me.

"Are you Lubo Peći?"

I nod, my voice failing me.

"Take all your stuff and follow me." He takes me to another large room. Another heavyset bald man in police uniform sits behind a large desk. He looks important. His large moustache, the same as Toma's, my barber in Zagreb, frightens me.

"Sit down on that chair," he says in a stern voice and points to the lonely chair in front of his desk.

"Do you know who I am?"

I shake my head from side to side unable to speak.

"OK. Now listen to me very carefully and do exactly as I say."

"I am the Chief of Police and I run this place. My spies are everywhere and if you don't do exactly what I tell you, they will report it to me and I will come after you."

"Now, after I leave, you are to count to ten. Do you know how to count?"

I nod my head up an down.

"I can't hear you."

My voice barely audible, I say, "Yes sir."

I am ready to cry, but think of Hanzi's words: 'Za inat' - to be brave and strong no matter what.

"OK. After you count to ten, you are to get up, take your belongings and slowly walk out of the police station. When you reach the end of the block you are to start walking faster. Do not run. Just walk as fast as you can and do not look back."

He winks, says "Good luck, kid," and leaves the room.

I count to ten as fast as I can, get up, pick up my backpack, and slowly walk through the exit door to the end of the block. The streets are deserted, with most people ready to sit down to their evening meals. I pick up the pace, and start to run to our house, as fast as my small legs can carry me. I reach our home out of breath, still trembling with the fear of walking alone through the streets. Aunt Babuš opens the door and before I could utter a sound embraces me. She begins to sob uncontrollably.

"Lubo, such a miracle. I am so happy you are OK."

Uncle Štefko embraces both Aunt Babuš and

me. He has a bright smile on his normally stern face. I see a few tears sliding down his cheeks. Hanzi and Greta come running from the other room and encircle our bundle, almost squishing me in the middle. They are all so happy that I am home again.

My joy at being home is quickly interrupted by the arrival of Uncle Štefko's peasant friend Mate who comes to take me to the neighboring village until everything settles down. He is an older man, with an unshaven face covered in grey stubble, white hair poking under his cap. He wears a loose white peasant shirt and a dark vest over it. I don't even have time to unload the backpack Aunt Babuš brought to the jail. I was hoping to spend the night in my bed and now I have to climb into the peasant's four-wheel cart pulled by a skimpy brown horse.

I sadly say my good byes to all.

"You be a good boy now. OK? You will be on Mate's farm just for a while." Uncle Štefko picks me up and tells me, "Lay down in the back of the cart. We don't want anyone to see you."

He covers me over my head with a blanket. Mate climbs in front and sits on the plank stretched between the two sides, takes the reins, snaps his whip, and yells, "Giddy up!"

The cart creaks and begins to move. Laying on the hard wooden surface, I can feel every bump and every rock on the way to the village. I peek through the crack of the cart, and watch the houses slowly fading away to be replaced by fields of corn and wheat. By the time we reach the village it is dark. I find comfort on a straw mattress in Mate's house and fall asleep.

That evening Uncle Štefko continues writing his letter.

. . .May 5th of 1943 was a sleepless night for us. Wondering and looking for salvation, I found a friend who advised me to contact an important government person who could successfully intervene. At 3 o'clock that afternoon I went to see him and to honestly report all that I knew and to express my feeling of indescribable grief and depression inside. This person, whose identity I must keep confidential, without any additional words, promised to intervene with two high military officers. He promised to have an answer for me, if I came back around 6 o'clock. I cannot describe how hard it was to wait for that time to pass. At 5 o'clock, he came to our house, but unfortunately I was not home. He left a message that he had a favorable answer and I should come immediately to see him. You can imagine my excitement after the tense wait. I went right away to see him. He could see from my face how depressed I was and immediately very carefully explained that he was successful in convincing the Chief of Police to exclude Lubo from the transport scheduled to leave two hours later. Neither Babuš nor I wish to ever go through such a brutal, frightening experience. Only the totally unexpected but desired surprise made up for what we went through. At 6:30 the little one came home, to be placed in our custody; we had complete responsibility for him. Even today I cannot clearly comprehend how successful we were in saving your son; Lubo, a single one among all the Jews, remained alive and free. In the meantime, I received your letter a few days ago, asking that we get ready to send Lubo to you. Babuš had already gone to Zagreb to try and get a permit from the authorities for him to go to you, and at the same time, to see a specialist regarding her sickness. She was not able to get the permit for safe passage from anyone and indicated that I should send him to Zagreb anyway.

Today I went to see the Chief of Police again to inquire if we could get a permit for the mentioned passage. He did not provide any direction, answer, or solution, regarding Lubo. He said that under no circumstance was I to turn the child over to anyone. I personally and the whole family was responsible for him. As the situation cools and if no one asks for Lubo, then there might be a way to send him to you. For the time being he is in no danger, and can remain with us in peace until we get the answer from the higher powers. Directly or indirectly, the Chief promised to let us know. He was very happy that he was successful in pulling Lubo out of the transport without any problems. He mentioned that if a permit later comes from the authorities, then everything would be quite different and he as well as we will have a cover.

At this moment, and obviously with the permission of the Chief of Police, Lubo is temporarily in a village with some good friends. During those two days and nights he was in jail Lubo was happy and had no special worries. When Greta asked him what he would like, he indicated that he would like his marbles. He is a child and does not seriously understand everything. His Catechism teacher, and all acquaintances love him very much and offered to intervene if anything else did not succeed. They are willing to pledge themselves for him to get him out. But, as you see, lucky for all, this was not necessary.

So now you know what the situation is. I believe strongly that we must and will find a way and method to legally send the little one to you. Who knows, it could be that the Chief of Police is wrong and that there is still danger that some day they would after all want to take the little one away. It would be best if he were not here, but for that we need a judicial permit, and I had to vouch with my own and my family's heads for him.
Babuš is in Zagreb again, and at this time don't know what she is doing to find a solution or suggestion for what to do.

One way, we thought, was to simply send the little one with Tatek to Zagreb and then have a lady take him with her across the border. While this might work, I am afraid and cannot afford to jeopardize my whole family. For that reason I think that the best way would be to find a way for us to send the little one legally to you.

I understand how these lines will affect you and I fully feel your pain, but I had to describe the situation just the way it is. It is very serious, and I hope that you will understand. We are very happy that despite all of the rejections of our requests, pleadings, and bowings, we finally did find people who understood us as human beings and came to aid us in saving the little one, who is safely under our care, though in a nearby village.

The Peći family is safe in Tešanj, hidden with some old friends. Just today, their friend was here with us and we sent them some foodstuff. Reže is in Osjek as a movie projectionist. He lives in a house on Glinska 84.

Otherwise we are well here with the exception of Babuš. I am worried about her. I wrote to her that unless it is absolutely necessary, she should not in this critical time subject herself to an operation, but I leave the decision to her.

I send you my warmest greetings.

Your,

Štefko

Lou Pechi

Vlado

Much happened over the next three weeks. While I was happy playing with my newfound friends in the small village, Aunt Babuš, Uncle Štefko, and many others were desperately trying to find a way to reunite me with my parents in Italy.

Their activities are best described in the letter, Uncle Štefko, wrote later in May to my parents in Italy:

5/28/1943

Dear Pirika and Pišta,

Yesterday Babuš arrived from Zagreb with Mrs. Milica Müller and after all the events we experienced yesterday and today, I am able to write this letter with much joy. All that was undertaken in Zagreb was to no avail and we were liberated from the tragedy that enslaved us over the last two weeks by Mrs. Müller's visit.

This evening at 10:30 she came to us after an evening spent with the Chief of Police with the announcement, "Children, roast the coffee, all is in order!"

I don't want to talk about myself, the

news made Babuš so happy, calm, dear; it brought a kind of satisfaction that cannot be put on paper by a mere pen. Babuš searched her mind how to say truthfully in words her extraordinary feelings and her gratitude to the person who spoke that sentence with such enthusiasm and joy, that I was somehow embarrassed by my feelings of pride. We had been successful in defeating and totally eliminating this tragedy from us!

Whatever little assistance and whatever material sacrifices were made, I don't intend to measure, but I just want to emphasize that May 4th, 1943 was a day of horror – and May 5th, 1943 a day of some relief – and May 22nd, 1943 a day of total calm and joy, thanks to the intervention of our dear Mrs. Müller who agreed to come with Babuš to Brod and personally arrange all that was in her power to free Lubo from the claws of the pending horror.

Now thanks to Dear God and the intervention of all who gave their words of pledge for our dear Lubo, everything will be in order, and you will in a few days have him in your midst and your embrace.

What a contrast between the feelings that burrowed into our souls a few days before and ruled until last night, and the feelings we feel today in our beings and our hearts.

Even Mrs. Müller is extremely happy that she was able to get the permission for the free passage of Lubo to you. We, as well, share our happiness with our guest.

And now about how all this came to be: a report of Mrs. Müller's visit to us and her evening with the Chief of Police in Brod. Babuš found out that the Chief of Police in Brod is the brother of one of her acquaintances in Zagreb, a certain Mr. Vinek, who immediately wrote a letter to his brother regarding some wrong done to the family Soldini during the past regime a few years before. And thanks to Mr. Vinek's letter, and Mrs. Müller's connection, the Chief of Police issued the permit for the freedom of Lubo. To all these good and kind people we must extend our thanks for the final success.

And finally, how will it all happen? Lubo is in a nearby village. This afternoon we sent for him and tomorrow morning they travel toward you. In a few days Babuš will go to the Chief of Police and present the report (naturally per his recommendations and instructions) that Lubo has disappeared. He will then file the report so that he is covered since he cannot be responsible for any accidental disappearance of a small child, while at the same time the report will cover us as well. So with the sacrifice of Mrs. Müller, Lubo and all the rest of us are safe.

I must say my dear Pirika, that there are always and everywhere honest people who are ready to offer help. My dear Babuš and I, will never be able to forget what Mrs. Müller and our friends did to enable Lubo to be excluded from the transport on May 5th, 1943 and remain here, which I feel, was more important than what happened today.

My dears! There is no reason to go into more detail about all the events, as hopefully there will be an opportunity for you two to personally get to see Mrs. Müller who can discuss with you in person all these events and report firsthand how we are here.

And now we eagerly wait tomorrow's day of departure and hopefully soon a letter from you indicating that he has arrived safely.

With him we are sending only some necessities, and later we hope to send the rest by Tatek. The most important is that we send him with just the necessities.

We received the other day 5 packages and that from February 6th, March 2nd, March 19th, March 26th, and April 2nd the last with chocolate, fountain pens, colors, rice, chocolate, and stockings for Babuš.

In one of the packages you asked if we have any needs. I would like to mention that we are interested in a harmonica with 120 harmonic bass notes. Mrs. Müller told us that this could be bought in Italy. Therefore, I specifically wish to ask, that she buys it for us, and we will request Tatek to exchange the Croat Kuna to Italian lire for you, or Mrs. Müller can send and Tatek can bring the harmonica. We would like to get this for the children. Babuš and I don't need anything. We are totally satisfied knowing that Lubo will be with you where he belongs.

In the future please write to our financial address and Tatek will bring your letters to us, and we will respond the same *way through Tatek.* <u>This has to be done this way</u>, *to protect all of our interests. If any unforeseen situation arises, we will use other personal addresses.*

I conclude with a wish that all is well with you.

Greetings,
Štefko

*   *   *

After Mrs. Müller's arrival in Brod, Uncle Štefko comes to the village and brings me home. I am so happy to see him. I was having such a good time in the small village, but missed my cousins Greta and Hanzi. I also didn't like the hard straw mattress and looked forward to sleeping in my own soft bed.

Uncle Štefko explains to me, "You will meet a nice lady, Mrs. Milica Müller who arrived last night from Zagreb. Tomorrow morning she will take you to Zagreb, and then on to Kolega and Mutika in Italy."

"During your trip you will have to pretend that you are her son Vlado. So if anyone asks you for your name you need to say 'Vlado Müller'."

"What is your name?" He asks me, to make sure I remember.

"Lu... I mean Vlado."

"What is your first and last name?"

"Vlado Müller," I respond with a bit more confidence.

"Remember also to call Mrs. Müller: Mom." I nod, as I think to myself. "She is not my Mutika."

Mrs. Müller has light brown wavy hair and too much makeup on her face. Her perfume has a strange strong smell of violets. She wears a flowery red dress, silk stockings with a black stripe in back, and brown high heel shoes. Mrs. Müller is a pretty lady, but Mutika is much prettier. Mrs. Müller's German accent reminds me of "Fräulein," who used to beat me until she got fired, and I get uneasy. I am not sure if I like her. *Why does she have to be my mother? Why do I have to be her son Vlado?*

All of this is coming too fast. I will be happy to see my parents, but sad to leave Hanzi and Greta. "Why must I have to leave again?"

Uncle Štefko explains more. "In a few days Aunt Babuš will go to the Chief of Police and report that you did not come home for two days and she fears that you have disappeared. He will then file a missing person report, so that he as well as we are covered."

I don't understand. *What does he mean by covered?* I picture the Chief of Police and Uncle Štefko each covered with big blankets. Besides, I am not missing. Aunt Babuš knows that Mrs. Müller is taking me to Italy. All of this is just too complicated, and I decide not to ask any more questions.

The next morning, with a sad face, I say goodbye to everybody. Aunt Babuš and Greta hug me and envelop my body as their sobbing rhythmically changes the pressure of their embrace.

Uncle Štefko and Hanzi, in their stoic way, admonish me to be strong.

"Pican, you are a big boy and need to behave like one. " Uncle Štefko says.

I see through their façade the sadness mixed with the happiness that my life was saved. My meager little suitcase is already packed. I put on my overcoat and Mrs. Müller holds my hand as we depart to go to the railroad station. Aunt Babuš and Uncle Štefko stay in the house and don't come to the station. They cannot be seen with me, since as soon as I am safely in Italy Aunt Babuš will report to the police that I am missing.

As I leave, I am no longer Lubo but a new boy, Vlado Müller, Mrs. Müller's son. I don't want to be Vlado Müller. She is not my Mutika.

We reach the station and are soon seated in the train compartment. I am quiet and reflect on what has happened during the last two weeks.

I wake up with a start as the conductor asks for our tickets. Mrs. Müller hands him our tickets. "Here are mine and my son Vlado's."

I want to burst out, "I am Lubo and not your son!" But I quickly remember that I have to pretend, so I check my feelings. I return the conductor's smile. The conductor leaves and I continue my private thoughts. I am a big boy. I must not be afraid. I have to be good. *It so unfair that I always have to leave places I love as soon as I get used to them. Why do I have to be what I am not? Why do I have to be who I am not?*

The train slows down as it approaches

Zagreb and the loud blast of a whistle interrupts my thoughts. When the train fully stops, we get off, take the underpass to the next platform and change trains to Rijeka that borders Italy's Fiume. The train is not crowded and I climb up onto the luggage rack and fall asleep to the rhythm of the wheels. I do not dream and am soon awakened by the screeching of the brakes as the train arrives to Rijeka. We get off the train and cross on foot the bridge into Italy.

The border guard examines our papers and by now, having fully stepped into Vlado Müller's shoes, I happily smile at the guard.

The sun shines brightly on a row of outdoor restaurants with white tables and chairs under orange and red umbrellas in front. People in bright summer clothes relax and eat ice cream or drink their coffee. Fiume looks so different from dull and dusty Brod. We walk a short distance to an outdoor café and spot a priest in a brown cassock and a blue beret, a stark contrast to the rest of the people, as he sips coffee at one of the tables. Mrs. Müller seems to recognize him and we approach his table. He looks a bit like Kolega, but his brown cassock reminds me of my confessor priest in Brod. Can I trust him?

He smiles, extends his hand, and speaks to me in German. "I am Father Stefano. You must be Lubo."

I cautiously shake his hand. He has difficulty pronouncing my name. The way he says it, sounds funny to me. I smile but don't correct him. I am glad that I don't have to be Vlado anymore, and happily accept his Italian accented version of my real name -

Lubo.

We sit down and Mrs. Müller orders a coffee for her and a lemonade for me. I quietly watch as Mrs. Müller tells Father Stefano all that happened in Brod. I see the shock on Father Stefano's face when he hears about my arrest.

"Oh my God! How could they do this to a small child?"

Father Stefano's smiles and his face relaxes when she tells him about my rescue. "A miracle! Thank God you got him out!"

My fears subside as I see that Father Stefano really cares about me.

Mrs. Müller finishes her coffee. She pulls her compact out of her large brown handbag on her lap, flips open the mirror cover, and with the round puff dabs some pink powder on each of her cheeks and nose. She pulls out a silver tube, twists the bottom, as a shiny red tip pops from the top. Intently staring in the mirror she purses and outlines her lips with short smooth motions.

"Oh! I almost forgot to give you this." Father Stefano interrupts, as he reaches into the folds of his cassock and pulls out a fat envelope.

"Thank you." Mrs. Müller returns the makeup into her purse and takes the envelope. She opens the flap close to her chest, to hide the contents from me. I can see her lips moving as she counts the contents of the envelope. When she finishes she hides the envelope in her big purse.

"I better get going, before I miss my train back to Zagreb." She hugs me, and some of the face powder rubs off on my cheek. "I am so happy you will be with your parents soon. Good bye." She departs and I wipe off the powder from my cheek.

Father Stefano asks "Are you hungry?" and I nod "Yes."

"Well you have to try something Italian. It is called a 'Panini' – or little bread sandwich."

He calls the waiter and orders it in Italian, a new language for me.

The waiter brings a plate with a flat round toasted bread roll sandwich. I bite into the soft warm bread crust, and taste the salty Prosciutto ham. It is delicious. Father Stefano delights in watching me eat.

"What do you think? Is it good?" he asks me.

My mouth still full, I nod and keep on munching.

After paying the waiter, Father Stefano and I board the short train ride to Treviso.

We spend the hour-long ride in conversation. He is delighted when I say, "I took Catechism classes and just had my first holy communion."

I carefully avoid the embarrassing confession question the priest asked me in Brod.

"That is so good. You are such a mature boy. I am really proud of you. What did you like the best in your Catechism classes?"

"My favorites were the Bible stories and the miracles Jesus performed."

"Maybe he performed one just recently," Father Stefano says.

The train pulls into the Treviso station and I

spot my parents waving at me on the platform. Kolega wears his fine suit and Mutika is in her nicest dress. I run to them as soon as we get off the train, jumping into the Kolega's outstretched arms. I can smell his aftershave that mixes with the familiar smell of Mutika's perfume. They both hold me for a long time and comment, "You got to be really heavy." Kolega puts me down, and steps back to look at me.

"My, how much you have grown. You are such a big boy."

Mutika picks me up again. Tears of joy streak her makeup as she holds me tight, "I am so happy to see you. I am so happy to see you," she keeps repeating. "I can't believe how much you have grown. You are such a big boy."

Father Stefano stands to the side with a broad smile of pleasure on his face. We all leave the station and walk a few blocks to the villa my parents share with their friends.

CLOUDY

Treviso - Uncle Marci, Mutika and Kolega

Venice – Piazza San Marco

Rome – Via Barberrini

Split – Partizan *Kolega*

Lou Pechi

Treviso Villa

The white villa stands like a wedding cake surrounded by a beautiful garden with a crown of iron fencing. Seated on chairs, surrounding a table laden with coffee cups, white plates with morsels of cake, a group of men and women dressed in pajamas enjoy the afternoon sun. When they see us they all get up and cheer and clap their hands. They converge on me like a flock of pigeons upon a handful of crumbs. I am overwhelmed by the hugs and kisses as they express their joy of seeing me. My arrival is a small victory for them.

I recognize in the group Uncle Milan, my boating friend in Juan Les Pins and earlier, my tormentor when I was four years old in Zagreb. My parents frequently hosted parties in our apartment Uncle Milan would always chase me around the house threatening me, "I will cut off your 'Pisher'." One day, I had enough, and decided not to run away any more. In front of our assembled guests, I dropped my pants, grabbed my 'Pisher', and shouted in an angry voice, "Here it is! Go ahead! Cut it off!"

Our guests roared with laughter. After that he never teased me again. We became good friends. I was glad to see him again.

After a few days, I started wearing my pajamas every day too. I don't have to get dressed; I and the other residents are not allowed to leave the villa. Most of the days Kolega and I walk around the garden, exploring. We discover a beautiful cobweb, small droplets of dew glistening in the morning sun. Kolega catches several live flies, congregating around the ever-present crumbs on the large table in the front yard and gently places one of them on the fine threads of the spider's web. The fly, stuck on the fine silvery strands, struggles to get free, and sends its vibrating messages across the whole web. A black spider emerges from the center of the web and scurries to the rippling source of the vibrations. Efficiently and with great speed he grabs the fly with his front legs and spins it as wings, legs, and the head quickly disappear into a silvery cocoon. He attaches the cocoon to the web, and returns to the center of his kingdom. The web, still again, sparkles in the afternoon sun, and awaits the next victim.

We feed the spider every day, and each day I hope the fly will break loose and escape its inevitable fate. It never happens.

I am not very interested in the endless card games the adults play, and busy myself with chasing and feeding the several chickens in the yard. The big rooster, who dominates the hens, follows me around the yard, and is not afraid to peck and eat the bread out of my hand. I name him: 'Kuku-riku' after the sound he makes each sunrise. One day the adults decide to feed 'Kuku-riku' as well. They soak bread in brandy that they sip throughout the day, before they feed it to 'Kuku-riku'.

"Why do you soak the bread in the brandy?" I ask them.

"Oh, it makes it easier for him to swallow." Uncle Milan responds. I see him wink at the rest of the people.

"Is he teasing me again?" I wonder.

After all the bread is gone, 'Kuku-riku's walk slowly changes. His proud strut becomes a wobbly balancing act on each of his legs as he tries to walk a straight line. The group laughs at every step the poor rooster takes.

I laugh as well, but miss his proud strut.

On Sunday morning, my parents tell me to get dressed in my nice clothing.

"Are we going to church?" I ask.

They burst out laughing.

"No, every Sunday, we have to report to the 'Questura' – the Italian police," my father explains. "We are 'Internati di Guerra' or interned because the war. The Italian government wants to make sure we have not left the town."

What does 'interned' mean? We are not in prison. We are in a nice villa.

A leisurely stroll through town and we reach a large old building, and climb a wide staircase to the second floor. Many of our friends are already in the room. Holding small china cups of espresso coffee they are engaged in lively conversation with each other and the chief of police. This is different than the mass I was required to attend in Brod. There, only the priest talked and the congregation was allowed only occasionally to answer in unison whenever the priest demanded it. I like reporting to the police much better.

The chief of police taps his spoon on the coffee cup and demands attention from all.

"I have some good news for all of you," the chief says. "There has been a revolt against Mussolini by his military Chief of Staff Badoglio. Mussolini has been deposed and arrested. You are at liberty to travel throughout Italy and do not have to report to the police any more. You are free."

"You mean we can travel to Venice or Rome?" Kolega asks.

"You can to go wherever you desire."

The room explodes in cheers. "Sloboda! Sloboda!" Freedom! Freedom! Everyone shouts.

"This calls for a celebration," Kolega says and leads us to a local restaurant. During the meal Kolega and Mutika discuss our next move.

Mutika proposes a plan. "Now that Italy has surrendered to the Allied forces, the American fleet should be in Venice any day. We should move to Venice as soon as possible."

Within a few days Mutika finds a small apartment there, and we pack our meager possessions, to become residents of Venice.

Our new city is quite different from Treviso. I don't have to stay in the house, as I did in Treviso. All of Venice is my playground. I roam and explore the small alleys, divided by boulevards of water, crisscrossed by round bridges, which provide me with a wonderful playground. Pretty soon I learn several ways to get to the Piazza San Marco, the large main square of Venice. Almost every day, we go to the Piazza. My parents and their friends sit in the outdoor cafe and sip their small cups of espresso, while I feed the flocks of pigeons on the square. The pigeons are not afraid of me. I open my hand, full of breadcrumbs, and they alight on my head, shoulder, and arm, as they peck the palm of my hand. They tickle me and I laugh in delight.

Each day we expect that the Americans will arrive, but there are none in sight.

One day, as we emerge from one of the alleys leading to the square, my parents stop in shock. I look past them to see soldiers and officers sitting at our tables in the square as they leisurely sip their coffee and smoke cigarettes. They wear the same uniforms as the two German officers who billeted in our apartment in Zagreb. Maybe Hauptman Otto is sitting with them.

"They are not the Allied soldiers we expected. They are Germans," Kolega says. "What happened to the American Fleet? What is going on? Something is not right."

We immediately turn around and don't go to the café. That evening, after long discussions of what to do, my Mutika says, "If the Americans are not coming to us, we should go toward them."

By that time, she explains, the Allies occupied Sicily and most of Southern Italy. "Rome should be liberated very soon. It would be the best if I went first, and, after I find a place for us to stay you follow me."

The next day she leaves, and, a week later, a letter arrives from her. She tells us the address of the apartment she's found. Once again Kolega and I pack our things and book a sleeper compartment. This time we depart for Rome.

Rome - Corso Trieste

The steady clinkety–clank of the wheels, that put me to sleep earlier, begins to change its beat. Gradually each clank is followed by an increasing pause as the train slows down and approaches Rome. Spring blooms mixed with the charcoal smoke of the engine waft through the open window.

I open my eyes and look past Kolega at the changing view of low brown houses, wooden sheds, green trees, and gardens that slowly melt into tall apartment buildings, factories, chimneys belching smoke, railroad cars standing on the empty tracks, all to be swallowed by the large glass dome of the railroad terminal. With a screech and a bang the train comes to a stop. I wonder if Mutika is waiting for us at the station.

We unload our suitcases. A uniformed bellboy in a red jacket wearing a matching round red hat with a strap under his chin, piles them onto a large cart, which he wheels to the entrance of the station. We trail behind, until he unceremoniously dumps the load on the curb and extends his hand, palm up. Kolega pays him and says, "I don't see any taxis. It must be because of the gas shortage."

Several tricycles, with a square platform cart in front, are lined on one side of the street. Kolega hails one of these. The man mounts the seat and pedals toward us. The suitcases barely fit on the small platform; we follow on foot.

It is almost an hour before we reach the top of a long boulevard — Corso Trieste. I'm tired. Kolega picks me up and sets me on top of the suitcases. The man lets the bike coast down the hill toward number 140, as the breeze cools my sweaty face. With nothing but the open street in front of me, I feel like I'm the one directing the bike.

Ahead on the curb Mutika is waiting, and waving at me. I'm so happy to see her. When the bike stops I jump off and run to embrace her. Kolega catches up and we all embrace, happy to be together again.

The apartment Mutika found is bright and sunny. It is on the corner of the second floor, with three bedrooms, a dining room and a sitting room. There are no decorations on the white walls. Several scattered darker square outlines, with nail holes on top, are the only evidence of recently removed paintings. A balcony on one side overlooks a large open field; the other balcony faces the street. What a difference from the dark, musty, and damp room we left behind in Venice.

At dinner that evening Mutika tells us, "I rented this apartment through a lawyer. It belongs to a Fascist high official, who escaped to Switzerland after Badoglio's revolt against Mussolini. He and his family left all their valuables in the maid's locked room which we are not allowed to open."

"If the apartment belongs to a Fascist, we should be safe here," Kolega says. I think he means that as a kind of joke but I am not sure.

The apartment is crowded. Our friend, Uncle Slavko, occupies one bedroom. Mutika, Kolega, and I sleep in the second bedroom, while Uncle Marci sleeps on the sofa in the living room. Of course, one other room is locked and contains items we are not supposed to use.

The next morning, Uncle Marci, who is handy with tools, jimmies the lock to the forbidden room. We open the door. The room is dark and smells musty. I feel like Ali Baba entering the cave of the Forty Thieves. I am speechless and keep repeating "Wow! Wow!" as my eyes dart from object to object.

Big paintings framed in shiny gold frames lean against the walls. Two lacquered tables hold piles of fine china plates and cups. A large mirror reflects a narrow sunbeam that shines through the small window. A sculpture of a couple, in loving embrace, stands next to a marble nude female torso. Two granite heads seem to look at them. Several tall stacks of books, lined up on one side, rise like city blocks filled with miniature buildings.

We bring the paintings out of the room. "This one should go here. And that small, goes there, " I tell Uncle Marci. He covers each darker square on the walls to gradually conceal all the evidence of the removed paintings.

We carry the books and fill the empty bookcase in Uncle Slavko's room.

I'm intrigued by their smooth leather bindings and begin reading the shiny gold engraved titles on the spines. The mysterious names:

Gulliver's Travels, A Tale of Two Cities, Oliver Twist, The Prisoner of Zenda, Robinson Crusoe and many others, make little sense to me. Curious, I open a random page of *Gulliver's Travels* and start reading about a large man pinned down to the earth by many tiny strings. Each strand of his hair is tied to a small stake in the ground and he can barely lift his head and see a small six-inch man standing on his chest, a tiny bow and a sword in his hand. Like the fly in the spider's web in the Treviso villa, his own hair pins him down. How odd? How did he get there? Does a place like that really exist? I cannot put the book down. I want to find more, and flip to the beginning and start to read. My Italian is not very good, but the story emerges as I stumble over the obstacles of unknown words that, like large boulders strewn in my path, block my progress. It gets late. Mutika takes the book away, "Bed time! You can continue reading tomorrow morning. Good night!" and puts me to bed.

I lay in bed, picturing the giant man who after being tied by the little people, finally befriends and helps them. I can't wait for tomorrow, to find out what happens next.

The next morning I dress in a hurry, swallow my breakfast, brush my teeth in two strokes, and finally return to Gulliver's imaginary world to spend the rest of the day with him.

I'm not allowed to play with the other children on the street since we don't have proper documents and the Germans, who now occupy all of Rome, randomly block a street block and check identification cards. But, the four walls of the apartment cannot hold in my imagination. Over the next several months, with my guides — Dickens, Dumas, Victor Hugo, Jules Verne and others — I travel the sewers of Paris, the slums of London, sail the Caribbean on pirate ships, and dive with Nemo to the depths of the ocean.

I am particularly fascinated by Dumas' book: *The Count of Monte Cristo*.

In this story, the hero is wrongfully imprisoned, escapes from jail, and acquires a large fortune, which he uses to take revenge on the men who destroyed his life. The story reminds me of my own arrest in Brod. I really don't know who reported me then and wonder if I could ever take revenge on them if I found them.

The scene in *Oliver Twist* where small Oliver is forced by Fagin to enter a window and open the front door for him in an attempted robbery, reminds me of when Hanzi pushed me into the rectory basement to steal the ham, sausages and wine. I did not get caught, like Oliver did. I feel sorry for Oliver, left orphan at an early age, and glance up at Mutika and Kolega, to make sure they are still there. I am so lucky to be with them.

Each evening we turn on the radio and listen to the latest news. We wait for the BBC signature — the four opening notes of Beethoven's Fifth Symphony — Bah-bah-bah-boom! — followed by a formal British voice: "This is the British Broadcasting Service."

It is against the law to listen to foreign radio transmission, so we move the receiver away from our neighbor's common wall to the farthest room. After the war, we find out that our neighbors did the same with their radio. We huddle around the dim dial, volume turned low, straining to hear the latest news:

> The Allied forces, in their advance toward Rome, are pinned down in the valley below Monte Cassino. The Germans have fortified the hillside fortress, using the monastery and the church as shelter. Our brave forces are regrouping for the delayed advance and capture of the German fortifications.

We listen to the news as if it were a football match. We cheer each success and boo every failure of the Allies. To our great disappointment, tonight we learn that the Allied team is unable to advance.

The only safe place we dare to venture is the Opera, which to the Italians is more sacred than the Vatican. The Germans are afraid that if they impose any restrictions on this Italian shrine, the result would be a major riot.

We sit high up in the upper Galleria. I can almost touch the painting of the galloping horses on the ceiling brightly lit by the chandelier in the center. Steep sloping rows of seats are crowded with casually dressed audience. Their loud conversations across several rows are punctuated by constant hand gestures. Heavyset women, their button-up dresses stretched between their spread knees, fill the narrow gallery chairs as they munch on large hunks of fresh bread. Stocky men, dark beard stubble on their unshaven chins, sip wine from round, straw- encased Chianti bottles. The smell of prosciutto and salami fills the air. The German soldiers and officers sit on the bottom floor and in the surrounding loges, their grey uniforms contrast the red velvet chairs and curtains.

The lights dim. To thunderous applause the conductor takes his stand in front of the orchestra. He waits until the last cough subsides and silence fills the hall. The conductor finally raises his arms, baton in his right hand, and lowers them as gentle notes of the "Aida" overture rise from the orchestra pit to float like a soft mist up to the galleria on top. A sweet melody envelops us all.

The curtain parts to a brightly illuminated scene of ancient Egypt. Men, draped in colorful vestments, strap-sandals on their feet, and garlands in their hair mill around the square. Women in see-through skirts, with gold tiaras in their long hair, and bracelets way up their arms, move gracefully through the crowd. A heavyset man, wearing a golden robe, sings about his future conquest and victory over the enemy. I don't care much about his singing. I'm trying to figure out how they make the buildings and the blue backdrop sky look so real. My interest grows with each change of scenery. The opera progresses to the court scene and ends with the final scene in which Radames and Aida, buried inside the pyramid burial crypt, gasp for their last breath. The small tomb takes me back into the Brod jail. The walls close in on me. I gasp for air. I feel sick.

I want to scream, "Help!"

The big red curtain comes down. The audience applauds. I am back.

The next day Kolega helps me build a small theater from some discarded packing boxes. I make a curtain from scraps of material and connect a battery to a small light that illuminates the stage. I cut out some figures from old postcards and prop them up so they stand on the stage like small actors. I sell the crudely hand printed entrance tickets to my parents, to Uncle Slavko, and Uncle Marci.

The next evening is the grand opening of Lubo's Opera Theater with the premiere performance of *Gulliver's Travels*. The scene opens, as Gulliver is getting ready for his trip.

His mother cautions him: "Be careful and make sure you brush your teeth every day. Here is the lunch bag I packed for you."

Gulliver gets into a tiny paper boat, floating over cardboard blue waves, that I pull across the stage by a small string. The next scene shows an oversized Gulliver lying on a grass mound as two small paper figures bind him with white threads. He wakes up and shouts: "Help me! I can't move."

"If you promise to be good, we will untie you," the small man says.

"I will be good," Gulliver promises and the men untie him. They all dance, clap their hands, and sing in unison "We are happy! We are free!"

The curtain descends. My small audience applauds enthusiastically; it is a great success.

Being in the three-bedroom apartment does not bother me; I keep busy exploring the extensive library, refining my small theater, and playacting the wonderful stories.

Eventually Mutika finds out that we can get false documents from a man who came with the retreating Germans from the island of Capri in the south and opened his false identity business in Rome. One can go to him, and for several thousand lire and a photograph, he will change your identity. Instantly I become a native of Capri. My new name is 'Beniamino Bellini'. I like the sound of my new name. In Italian 'Bene' means 'Good' and 'Amo' means 'Love'. It is almost like my official Croat name 'Ljubomir' - 'Lover of Peace', where 'Ljubo' means 'Love' and 'Mir' means 'Peace'.

I feel even better when Kolega explains, "In Hebrew, 'Ben' means 'Son' and 'Yamin' means 'Right', so you are my Kolega – my right hand."

With the false documents in hand we become brave and occasionally venture out. Kolega and I ride the bus back to our apartment. He looks puzzled and preoccupied.

"What is the matter Kolega?" I ask.

"I forgot which is my first and which is my last name."

He pulls out his new identity card reading aloud "Amadeo Gualtieri". Either one could be a first or a last name. I'm thankful my first and last names are not easily mixed up.

The next week, Uncle Slavko takes me to the barber in our neighborhood, who, just like my barber in Zagreb, sits me on a plank laid across the two armrests. I am afraid of the sharp razor. I don't like getting haircuts. The barber asks me my name, and I nervously reply, "Beniamino".

"What a beautiful name you have. How old are you?"

"Nove – Nine," I reply in perfect Italian.

"Che bel ragazzo!" What a beautiful boy, he comments to uncle Slavko, who nods his head, afraid to speak, afraid to expose his poor Italian.

"Pura razza Italiana!" Pure Italian race, the barber adds. Little does he know that my real name is not Beniamino, and that I am not Italian, but Jewish as well.

Slavko winks at me, as if he is reading my thoughts.

Rome - Pensione

One day I overhear Uncle Slavko talking to my parents after he returns from another evening of gambling at Hotel Baglioni.

"I have some good news, and I have some bad news. The good news is that last night I got lucky and won a large sum of money in a poker game. The bad news is that if I don't to pay them 10,000 lire and return the money I won in the game, the losers will report me to the police."

Kolega looks worried. "How are you going to pay them? You don't have that kind of money."

"Well, I told them that it will take me some time to get such a large amount of cash, and they agreed to meet here in a week. That will give us some time to move where they or the police can't find us," Slavko continues.

I think, "OH, No! We have to move again? I was so happy with my books, theater, and the calm I enjoyed in our sunny apartment. I don't want to move. Stupid Uncle Slavko."

The next day Mutika finds a small Pensione downtown Rome, near Piazza Barberini. In order not to arouse any suspicion we take only our bare necessities and leave our Corso Trieste apartment in separate groups. Mutika and Uncle Slavko leave alone one day and Kolega and I follow the next day. I can't take my books nor my little theater with me.

Why do we have to move again? I am so tired of moving.

The Pensione is on the fourth floor of a five-story building. It is right next to Piazza Barberini, where several large boulevards converge on the Bernini Triton fountain in the center. We are crowded into two small rooms, with windows overlooking a garage on the street below.

Next week Uncle Slavko, after meeting with the men at our apartment tells us, "When I met with the men, I told them that I tried, but was unable to round up such a large sum of money and they will have to turn me in. They were not very happy when they left."

A few days later a summons arrives requesting that Uncle Slavko report to the police. We all plead with him not to go, but he decides to go anyway. I beg him, "Please, don't go. They will shave your head, like they shaved mine in Brod."

He laughs. "Don't worry. I will be back."

And sure enough, a few hours later he is back; his head still covered by his brown hair.

He tells us, "I met with the police inspector who kept looking at a letter on his desk. When the inspector left the room for a moment, I picked up the letter and read it. It had all the correct information about me: my real name – Slavko Brenner, that I am Jewish, and was a captain in the old Yugoslav army. I replaced the letter and after the inspector returned, I told him the truth. The inspector told me that he is very busy right now and that I should return in a week. I think he just wanted to let me go."

Despite Uncle Slavko's insistence on returning, this time we are able to convince him not to go back. Mutika is happy. Kolega just shakes his head. I am so glad he listened to us.

In the next few days, I discover the large expanse of the roof above the fifth floor and claim it as my domain. I put on Mutika's combing cape, and leap from building to building over the whole city skyline, from Saint Peter's to Castel Sant'Angelo, and all the way to the Coliseum. I can fly! I am Superman!

In the evenings we huddle in front of the radio volume turned low and listen to the BBC news:

> This morning the Allies landed at Anzio beach to open a new front and encircle the fortifications of the German forces in Monte Cassino and continue their advance North toward Rome.

But days drag on until the afternoon of June 4th, when an eerie stillness descends on the streets of Rome. We watch through the curtained windows; silence rules over the empty street below. The roar of a solitary motorcycle interrupts the calm; it pulls up to the garage across the street. The German soldier in the sidecar gets out, peeks into the garage, rattles the grating, and gets back in. They roar off and all is quiet again.

On the horizon the setting sun outlines the shadow of an airplane as it seeds the ground with distant explosions. We watch and wait. The sun disappears, dusk follows, and night hides the city. Behind every unlit window eyes scan the empty streets below afraid to disturb the dark silence, afraid to step out. The air is full of anticipation. Have the Germans really left? Are they hiding on the rooftops? When are the Allies going to arrive?

The silence is slowly disturbed by a distant hush, like a far-away waterfall. It gradually grows into a loud roar as the flow fills the nearby streets and spills into the main square. Two single files of Allied soldiers, dusty green uniforms, round helmets, backpacks on the stooped shoulders, rifles held in weary arms, slowly walk, step after tired step. They are swallowed by a happy smiling, cheering, clapping, shouting crowd. Rome is liberated!

We turn the radio up to full blast and hear the announcement:

> The people of Rome have crowded onto the streets to welcome the victorious Allied troops. The first American soldiers, members of the 5th Army, reached the center of Rome after encountering only dogged resistance from German forces on the outskirts of the city.

"Mutika, please, can I go down and see the soldiers?" I beg her to let me join the cheering crowd, but she refuses.

"You can't go down. You will have to wait until the trucks and heavy machinery arrive. I am afraid the Germans might ambush the soldiers." She hardly finishes her sentence when we hear several shots. We run to the window and see the crowd fleeing in all directions.

"I told you it is an ambush." Mutika is always right.

We soon learn that the weary soldiers, mobbed by the happy throng tossing flowers at them, fired the shots into the air to disperse everyone. Finally some trucks full of soldiers arrive and Mutika lets me go out. The soldiers on the trucks throw down candy bars. I catch as many as I can grab, fill my pockets, stuff the rest into my shirt, and finally return home to savor my booty. The chocolate melts in my mouth. Freedom is sweet.

Next week we return to Corso Trieste. I abandon my books and my trusty fictional friends, to join the gang of children playing on the street. They welcome me, "What is your name? We saw you in the window. How come you stayed in the house all this time and never came down to play with us?"

I tell them, "I am Lubo. I am Yugoslav. I am Jewish. We were hiding from the Germans."

They are impressed that I had to hide from the Germans. They ask me, "What does Jewish mean?" I shrug my shoulders. I really don't know.

That summer, Gian Carlo, his little brother Alberto, the twins Gemelli, Franco, Massimo, and I conquer and declare the neighborhood streets our domain. We play endless games of hide and seek till evening or hunger drives us home. We divide into two teams and play soccer or war against each other. Our extended fingers become our guns, capable of inflicting mortal wounds. When one is shot he must writhe in agony and lay on the ground. Our common enemies are the 'Portieri' the porters, who sit by the entrances to the houses and don't allow us to play there.

We form a secret society we call, "The Black Leopards," and I compose our hymn:

```
INNO DEI LEOPARDI NERI

Leopardi tantoneri
Corron com esuli pensieri
Etiran con la fionda dei sassoni neri

  Contro i portieri
conr certi bastoni veri
Dando botte da maestri severi
     MORTE AI PORTIERI
```

Hymn of the Black Leopards
Leopards so black
Run like exiled thoughts
Shoot with slingshots black stones

Against the porters.
Beat them with real sticks
With severe masters' blows.

DEATH TO THE PORTERS

We dare each other to visit the catacombs. For a few lire, a priest guides us through the dark corridors we enter from the side of a small church. A flickering candle in the priest's hand illuminates the path ahead. Human skulls and bones appear from the darkness only to fade into darkness as we pass by. We follow each other, trembling, clinging together as if to get courage from each other, only to emerge from the darkness into the bright sunlight and boast how we were not afraid of the dark.

One day, while we are playing, Massimo finds a nicely wrapped package tied up with a big bright ribbon in front of a house belonging to a former Fascist collaborator. Hoping that it contains something good — cake or chocolate — we carry it to our hideout in one of the back yards. We untie the ribbon and open the package. A foul, stinking, smell rises from the box as we find that the chocolate we expected is just a pile of human excrement on a cardboard tray.

"I know what to do with this," I tell my friends. "I will smear this on the chair of the portiere who always chases us away."

We watch when he leaves his chair and I run past, turn the paper tray over, and smear the brown mess on the seat. We celebrate our victory, not knowing that a lady watched us from the window, and told the portiere who was the culprit.

I arrive home, not suspecting anything. Mutika is dressed in her finery, hair all done, nails freshly lacquered, ready to go out. "Who smeared the shit on the nice portiere's chair across the street?" she asks.

"I don't know."

I am puzzled how she knows about it.

"It wasn't me." She starts to spank me until I start to cry.

"I did. I am sorry. We found the package and didn't know what to do with it. That portiere is so mean."

"So, you had to smear it on his chair? Did you?"

She shakes me and notices that one of her freshly lacquered nails broke when she hit me. I get an additional spanking for the broken nail.

"You are not allowed to go out to play with your friends and will be confined to the house until you learn your lesson."

I wonder what lessons I have to learn.

During the next two weeks my only communication with my Leopard friends is through a basket I lower from the balcony as we exchange toys and candy.

Rome after the war is an endless playground for a ten-year-old, and when I am finally allowed out of the house I explore it all. Places I read about in the apartment library during my confinement spring up in their full glory. The Coliseum where I staged imaginary sea battles and fights between armored men throwing nets over each other, and men fighting ferocious beasts—reveals the ruins of passages underneath the stage that once was the sand filled floor of the arena.

I walk over the bridge to Castel Sant'Angelo, and follow the wide boulevard to St. Peter's square. The long curving rows of stone columns, like opening arms, seem to summon everyone to enter the basilica. I walk the long Vatican corridors lined with paintings, maps, sculptures, icons, ceilings crowned by frescoes, and open windows on each side, that connect to the magnificent Sistine Chapel.

The large Allied trucks keep to the periphery of Rome and unless lost, do not wander the downtown streets. One morning such a truck, the driver perched on his seat high up in the sky, comes to a screeching halt in front of our house. The driver descends in a leap from his throne and proceeds to speak to me in pidgin Italian. "*Come*? How do I get to? I mean: *andare* to Foro Mussolini?"

I know the place is a sports complex that has been turned into an Allied military base. I respond in perfect English. "You have to turn right and take a left on Via Nomentana and follow it all the way to the end."

His eyes open wide in amazement that this little Roman boy speaks to him in his native tongue.

"How come you speak such good English? I am John. What is your name?"

"I am Lubo. We are Yugoslav refugees and I learned English in kindergarten."

"Pleased to meet you? Why don't you come with me and show me the way?"

He lifts me up on the seat next to him. Over the truck's long hood, the street below seems far away, almost as if we are in a low-flying airplane. The roar of the motor changes pitch as he shifts the gears, letting the machinery move forward on the large rubber tires. As we sail above the streets I am so proud. I feel like the captain commanding a large ship. We stop in front of a large gym-like building and the driver lifts me down to the ground. John takes me inside into a large kitchen and sets me at a table in the middle.

"This is Lubo. He is a Yugoslav refugee whom I picked up in downtown Rome. He speaks English."

John introduces me to the cooks in large white aprons who congregate around me and bring plates of food, commanding me to eat.

"I am not really hungry," I say, but to them I am just a starving little war orphan who needs to be fed.

John pulls out a wallet full of family pictures and shows them to the cooks. "Lubo looks exactly like my youngest son Tom."

They nod in agreement. He excuses himself, and tells me he will be back soon. Meanwhile I pick through the piles of meat, potatoes and unfamiliar food. The cooks bring me a huge plate of ice cream - for that I find plenty of room in my tummy.

The driver returns from the PX with a shopping bag full of hard candy.

"This is your reward for being my guide."

We climb back into the truck and retrace our way until he deposits me back in front of the house. I run to Mutika smiling, my huge treasure in my hands.

"Where have you been?" she scolds me. "You were gone more than four hours. I was frantic with fear."

"A nice soldier picked me up in his big truck and I showed him how to get to Foro Mussolini."

"Going away with a stranger, in a truck, of all things! You are never to do this again."

"But Mutika, nothing happened. They fed me and I ate a whole bowl of ice cream. And look at the bag of candy he gave me."

Candy is better than money; I can trade it with my friends for chewing gum, chocolate, or toys.

I enjoy my freedom, and have too much fun to notice that something is not right between my parents.

"I think that I will join the Partisans in Yugoslavia," Kolega says one night at dinner.

To which Mutika responds irritably, "Good riddance!"

I wonder what does she mean by that? I don't like it when my parents argue. A few days later Kolega leaves for Bari in the South, only to be transferred to the Partisan beachhead on the coast of Yugoslavia. With his knowledge of motorcycles and automobiles and his fluent German, he is quickly promoted to the head of the motor pool that uses German prisoners to perform all the repairs. Mutika, left alone in Rome, goes out almost every evening to parties given either by wealthy Italians for the Allied forces, or by Allied forces for the Italians.

I stay home, cooking my own supper. I become an expert on egg dishes, adding onions, meat, pasta, vegetables, or any other thing I can think of.

Frank, a dashing US Navy officer of Croatian descent, becomes Mutika's regular escort, and shows up regularly in his Jeep. After a while the Jeep remains parked overnight in the short driveway in front of our apartment house and Frank sleeps in the study. I like Frank. I like the white Navy uniform he wears whenever he and Mutika go out. He is much bigger than Kolega. He used to play football at USC. Frank brings me candy and chewing gum, the currency of the kids of Rome.

One night, I wake up to Frank's shouting from the study balcony. I run to the adjoining balcony to see what all the commotion is about. Below, several youths push Frank's Jeep as they try to start the motor. Frank, in his undershorts, holds his service revolver in his extended arm and points up to the sky. He shouts obscenities in Croatian. I think this is very funny; they don't understand what he is yelling, so they keep pushing the Jeep. A loud gunshot scatters them like mice.

The next day we load the Jeep with blankets and food and drive to Ostia, the nearby beach for a Sunday picnic. Jumping in the salty waves brings back memories of old times in Juan Les Pins. My swimming is not dulled a bit by the long absence from water. I float, dive, and ride the waves. The sun feels good and the food tastes great.

One day Kolega returns, wearing a brown British uniform, and a cap bearing a red star. He is a regular Partisan. I am proud of him. He has come back to take me to Zagreb. My grandma Omama has cancer - she is dying, and her last wish is to see me.

I don't want to go. I am having too much fun in Rome. I will miss my "Leopard" friends. I will miss Frank. I will miss Mutika. Why do I have to move?

Little do I suspect that ten years will pass before I see Mutika again.

Lou Pechi

SUNNY

Lou Pechi

Zagreb – The Return

Zagreb, July 15, 1945

Dear Mutika,

Kolega and I arrived safely in Zagreb last night. It took us only three days to get here from Rome and I already miss you. How are my friends in Rome? Here I don't have any friends, but next month I will start Junior High School and Kolega tells me that there I will meet some new friends.

Aunt Beba, Rožika, and Otata are fine and send their regards. Tomorrow we are going to visit Omama in the hospital.

Hope you are fine. I miss you very much.

Love,

Lubo

P.S. Give my regards to Frank.

The next day Kolega and I take the trolley to visit my grandmother Omama in the hospital.

We walk from the trolley up a winding path. Like a mother hugging its child the tall trees gently bend over and embrace the road. A soft breeze, smell of fresh grass and the sweet trees follows us, ruffling my recently combed hair.

I just turned eleven. I wear my good clothes, brown lace up shoes, topped by knee high socks, short suit pants, white shirt, and suit jacket. I carry a bouquet of fresh flowers, bought from a stall on the bottom of the hill. We approach a large white building and enter between two massive columns flanking the doors of the hospital. We are on our way to see Omama.

I imagine we, like the heroes of my comics, are on a mission to liberate Omama from the clutches of the evil doctor in the hospital who is keeping Omama against her will, having heavily sedated her. The bouquet of flowers hides two weapons: a potent sleeping potion with which we will overcome the doctor and a counteractive potion to the sedative the evil doctor is administering to Omama. After we rescue her we will have a big party at her house to celebrate our daring rescue.

We climb a curved marble staircase to the second floor. There is a long hallway on each side. We turn right. A row of white doors face closed windows across the hall, as if they were soldiers guarding the wide long hallway. On each door there is a big black letter. We enter door 'C'. Cancer in English begins with the letter 'C'. Could it be that they put Omama in that room because she has cancer? Isn't cancer a crab? Does she have one big cancer crab inside her grasping her liver in his claws and chewing on it, or are many small crabs crawling inside her body and devouring everything in sight.

Crabs remind me of earwigs and I am afraid of earwigs. When you sleep one of them could crawl into your ear and eat your brain with its pincers. Could the small crabs jump and crawl through my mouth, nose, or ear and eat my insides?

We enter the room and are confronted by two rows of white metal beds, with nightstands next to them. Patient's faces poke under white linen sheets. The ceiling, the walls, and even the floors are white. Except for the blue sky peeking in through the open wide windows everything is white. Even the carbolic smelling air feels white, the blue breeze from the windows powerless to give it color.

I hear from one of the beds a soft whisper," Lubo! Edesh gyermek!" It must be Omama. I rush over, my extended hand following the flower bouquet. I stop, but am not sure it is Omama. Her neatly braided hair now lies lifelessly on her shoulders. Only her shining eyes peak out of a droopy yellow face. She extends her hand and takes hold of me. Her hand is yellow and I can't see the familiar brown spots. She pats the bed and motions me to sit down. I hesitate. What about the cancer crabs crawling inside her body? What if the yellow rubs off and attaches itself to my body to turn me yellow too? Can just touching her pass the color on to me?

"Why are you so yellow?" I ask.

She just smiles, shrugs her shoulders, and embraces me. I close my eyes. I am back when I was four years old. I sit next to the warm wood stove. Smells of pastry baking, freshly brewed coffee, boiling cabbage, meat sauces, laundry bleach, and grilled onions fill my nostrils. Omama sings a sad song about Maritza who sat on a cold stone and cried about losing her parents and how she doesn't have anybody anymore.

"Ja sam Marica, nemam nikoga."
(I AM MARICA, I DON'T HAVE ANYONE)
"Oca nemam, majke nemam, ja sam sirota."
(NO FATHER, NO MOTHER, I AM AN ORPHAN)

"Will my parents die? Will I be an orphan?" I ask in a quivering voice and burst into tears. My tears fall on my grandma's yellow face as she consoles me that everything will be fine.

Ten days later, we do liberate Omama from the clutches of the evil doctor and lay her head on a cold stone of the big marble family grave in the 'Mirogoj', (Peace-garden) cemetery.

I am sad and miss Omama, Mutika, and all my Roman friends: Gian Carlo, his little brother Alberto, the twins Gemelli, Franco, and Massimo.

To comfort myself I visit all the old familiar places. I yearn for the warmth they gave me a long time ago. At Krešimirov Trg, only a block away from my new home, the small pool is now drained of its water. The sand box, still full of grey sand, brings back memories of tin soldier battles on the sand dunes. Fräulein sitting on the bench, waiting for her always-late boyfriend, flashes in my mind. I don't miss her.

I walk by our old apartment on Zvonimirova Ulica and glance at the empty balcony. My hobbyhorse Malen is not there. A Partizan soldier in a brown uniform, a cap with a red star on his head, shiny boots on his feet, stands at attention holding a rifle slung on his shoulder. He is guarding our apartment, now a military office. I walk by and give him a snappy salute.

"*Zdravo, Kolega*," I greet him.

Not a muscle on his face moves as his steely eyes stare past me into infinity.

I guess I should have used the new greeting I overheard the officials use:

"*Smrt Fašizmu! Sloboda Narodu!*" Death to Fascism! Freedom to the People!

Around the corner I am welcomed by the sweet smell of the linden trees as I march between them swinging my arms and lifting my feet high, like a soldier on parade.

The downtown streets are deserted, quiet, empty of the well-dressed men with dark fedoras, and stylish ladies in their colorful dresses and hats. I search for my traffic policeman friend in the center of the intersection. There is no traffic. The place he always stood is empty.

I speed up my pace past the red and white barbershop pole and with fearful fleeting glance search for Toma, the barber I hate. I am relieved; the sign on the doors reads "CLOSED."

On the main square the statue of Ban Jelačić riding high on his horse, pigeons perched on his sword, extends his right hand and points toward

Austria. He fought for freedom of Croatia from the Austrians and I can almost hear him saying now to the German soldiers, "Go back to Germany. The war is over."

The central market, next to my Montessori Kindergarten, is not in session and patiently awaits the morning crowds. I remember my excitement and trepidation climbing the steps, holding Mutika's hand when she took me there for the first time. I pass empty stands that look naked without the varied assortment of rich summer fruit, green vegetables, and rainbow colored flowers. Folded red umbrellas, point up to the sky, ready to unfurl and shelter the village vendors: women in red kerchiefs and men in black fedoras.

Mutika would be so happy to be here!

Tired and hungry, I return to our new apartment and am greeted by the wonderful smell of onions, cabbage, tomatoes, the aroma of *Sarma* – stuffed cabbage. Aunt Beba is preparing our lunch. She is such a great cook. I love the meals she makes.

Aunt Beba is Kolega's younger sister. She is the housekeeper, cook, cleaner, laundress, and boss of the household. She wears a faded housecoat all day, as she shuffles around the house in her felt slippers. Her white face, exposed to the sun only when she ventures out to shop at the central market, contrasts with her dark hair peeking out from her flowery headscarf.

She is the first to rise at six in the morning to awaken the two white geese locked in a small crate on the balcony. Still in my pajamas, I watch her as she picks up the geese by their feet, one in each hand and waddles from side to side, to bring them to the tiled entranceway. It is breakfast time. Aunt Beba sits on the floor and straddles the geese, one under each leg; their long necks, like whiting snakes, struggling to get loose. She grabs one of their heads with her left hand, parts the beak with her thumb and forefinger, and forces the mouth wide open. She reaches with her right hand into a pot full of corn soaked overnight in water. She takes a handful of corn, as water dribbles back into the pot, and fills the geese's gaping mouth. With the forefinger, she pushes the kernels into the throat and slides her hand down the white neck to push the bulging lump down into the stomach. Alternately she repeats the procedure with each goose, until all the corn is gone.

One morning, several months later, using two hands this time, Aunt Beba picks up only a single goose by the neck; its heavy body swollen by the daily corn meals, hangs heavily as wings flap trying to fly. A wide basin, with a sharp butcher's knife inside, sits in the usual place next to where the pot of corn used to be. She straddles the fat goose, same as every day, but instead of opening the yellow beak, she entwines the neck between her left hand fingers until it bulges out. She reaches for the knife and with a smooth swift stroke slices a red gash across the white neck. Life squirts out of the gap, as the goose squirms between Aunt Beba's legs, body growing limp, as the basin fills with the red blood. She picks the limp body by its feet and hangs it on a steel wire stretched on the balcony. A small red line traces its way from the open wound across the white neck down to the eyes on the head to drip-drip, into the basin below. The second goose follows the fate of the first one. Both are then dipped into a pot of boiling water and then plucked naked of their white feathers.

I think of 'Pig' and how sad I was to lose my friend whom I fed until he grew big and fat, only to be slaughtered, bathed in boiling water, and cut to pieces. I don't feel the same for the geese. I didn't even name them.

Two huge livers, fattened by the stuffed corn and baked in the oven, sit majestically in the metal pan. I can't wait till they cool to taste them. Aunt Beba slices the skin and fat from the geese and fills a pot on the stove. The heat dissolves the contents into transparent liquid goose fat, which Aunt Beba pours into empty jars so it will cool and turn white. She will use the fat the rest of the year to cook our meals.

That evening we have a delicious soup made from the yellow goosefeet, beaks and heads. After dinner the whole family sits in the parlor, stripping the dried feathers of their soft down, to be made into pillows and comforters. These geese gave their all to feed the family. Everything used up. Nothing is thrown away.

Once a year at the end of the summer it is cabbage-pickling time. Aunt Beba brings the waist high barrel, now empty of last year's remains and scrubbed clean, from the closet. She places it in the middle of the kitchen. She lays a flat shredder board, its sharp blade barely showing on top, across the rim. Aunt Beba, sleeves of her housecoat rolled above her elbows, slides a head of cabbage back and forth across the shredder. Cabbage strings fall like confetti into the barrel below. She sprinkles some rock salt, adds a few garlic cloves and several hot red peppers, and arranges several whole heads of cabbages on top. Then she proceeds to shred more cabbage. She repeats that several times until the barrel is full to the top. Throughout the year she will use the softened cabbage leaves to wrap around balls of meat and rice and make my favorite food – Sarma, stuffed cabbage rolls.

Most days, at two in the afternoon, Aunt Rožika, Kolega's youngest sister, arrives for lunch from her office. She wears a dark business suit, her hair neatly combed, cheeks rouged, eyelashes blackened, and lips shiny red. She flips off her high heels, flops down on the living room couch and perches her legs on the coffee table. Aunt Rožika is a clerk at the government labor union office near our house.

"Fix me a cup of Turkish coffee," she yells at Aunt Beba as she pulls from her large purse a pack of cigarettes and lights one with a flick of her lighter.

"Fuck the Communist Party," she exclaims through a puff of smoke. "They made me join the Party today. It was either becoming a Party member or losing my job. I really don't give a shit. What do I care?"

Aunt Beba scurries with the coffee, a worried look on her face; but Beba keeps quiet.

I giggle in the other room. Aunt Rožika is using cuss words I am not allowed to repeat. I wish I could say whatever I want. I wish I could be like her; I like her. Aunt Rožika is my friend.

"Please, can you read me the comics" I beg her. I miss reading my Italian comic books Mutika used to buy me in Rome. I don't know how to read the Belgrade newspaper comics, written in Cyrillic alphabet.

"If you tell me where Aunt Baba hid the apples I will read the comics to you."

I show her where Aunt Baba hid the apples, so I would be the only one who eats them. I reach inside the stove and give her a red apple. "Now will you read?"

Aunt Rožika munches on it, and with a full mouth, reads the comics to me.

The door to the small room behind the kitchen is always locked. This is the workshop where my grandfather Otata keeps his tools. I am not allowed in the room without him. Otata was a retired master machinist who worked for the Austro-Hungarian and later Yugoslav railroad. He tells me that he started working when he was the same age as me, thirteen. He had to sweep the machine shop floor for many years, before he was allowed to use the tools. He never smiles and is always stern, but I sense his love for me. I admire his big thick calloused hands, shaped by the metal he handled all his life. His hands are capable of making anything.

His bald head, surrounded by a short-cropped ring of white hair, glistens and reflects the small overhead light. He is bent over a V-shaped plank of wood; he presses a small piece of plywood with his left hand, as his right hand makes the jigsaw oscillate up and down. His gaze is fixed on the spot where the blade meets the thin blue line on the plywood, as he wills it to follow the prescribed path. I watch as the blade makes the full round of the plywood and a bone shaped piece pops out.

I ask him "What are you making?"

"A lathe," he replies.

"What is a lathe?"

"You will see when it's done."

Over the next few months, I sit on the small stool next to the worktable and watch him pop out an assortment of different shapes. He rounds some of the edges, glues some of the pieces together to form strange objects. He explains to me that these are molds for the sand castings he will take to the foundry he used to work in. There he will transform them into metal objects. Soon the cast iron twins displace the plywood shapes on his desk.

Like a hungry dog holding a bone, a metal vice replaces the V-shaped plank of wood and grips the iron shapes in its jaws. Otata, in deliberate movements, carves flat surfaces into the shapes. He carefully measures the smooth surfaces, marks lines with a sharp pointer, and hammers a punch where the lines meet. These points, he tells me will be used to drill holes, so that the pieces can be put together. He does not have the drill and will have to take the pieces to his friends in the machine shop. He will take the round pieces as well to carve teeth on their periphery and form gears for the lathe.

The assortment of various parts on the shelf next to the table keeps growing, I can't wait until to see the finished product and each day I keep asking Otata when he will put the lathe together.

"You have to have patience, my child," he tells me. "You have to have all the parts, each part must be exactly accurate, and only then, it is possible to put them all together to make a working lathe."

I watch him as he screws and bolts parts together, mounts the wheels, meshes the gears, turns the wheels by hand, connects the belt to the electric motor in the back, and finally turns on the electric switch. Gears bite into each other. Wheels turn in unison. The lathe joyfully roars a machine song, and comes alive. I think of the mechanical toys Kolega used to bring me from his trips to Austria. The large toothed wheels of the lathe, like the toy's smaller ones, mesh into each other, and the electric motor, same as the spring in the toy cars that drives the wheels, powers the lathe. I watch, my eyes wide open, a smile frozen on my face.

After he builds the lathe, he continues building a mechanical band saw and a small vertical drill. He uses these tools to build a line of wooden fire engines with electric lights, rubber wheels, and a mechanical ladder that can be extended several feet, by turning a small crank on the base.

To this day I still follow the lesson of the lathe my grandfather Otata taught me. Before I make any major decisions, I collect all the facts, make sure each one is accurate, evaluate them, and only then take any action. He was my guide.

Lou Pechi

Zagreb – Continued

I completed the fifth grade in Rome and am ready to start Junior High School in Zagreb. The Second Boys High School is near our house so I can walk to school every day. The two-story building occupies a whole block and snakes in a large "U" around three sides, leaving a large courtyard in the middle. Our classroom, next to the school entrance is bright and airy with large windows that overlook the street outside. My bench, which I share with another boy, is close to the front. That afternoon, walking back home from my first day at school, I spot another boy from my class and quicken my pace to catch up with him.

"Hi, you are in my class."

"Yes." He turns around and from his smile I can tell I will like him.

" I am Lubo. What is your name?"

"Boris. Boris Kolar."

"Pleased to meet you," I respond, as I have always been taught. "Where do you live?"

"On Anke Butorac Street 8."

"Great. I am in number 7, right across the street from you. I just moved here. My mother lives in Rome, but I will join her soon."

I am glad Boris lives so near me.

"I live with my mother, baby brother, and grandmother," he says. "My father was killed in the war."

"Sorry to hear that. Maybe tomorrow, we can walk to school together." He agrees.

I am happy. I have found a friend.

From then on we not only walk together to school, but also spend time in each other's houses studying and playing. Boris is a great artist. He can copy any of the comics I brought from Italy. He teaches me how to draw Mickey Mouse and other Disney characters. Boris is a good student and gets high grades in all the classes we take. He introduces me to Ivo and Juro. All four of us are top students and we hang out together all the time. Mostly we call each other by our last names: Boris is Kolar, Ivo is Likar, and Juro becomes Valent, his last name Valenteković, which we consider too long. I am happy that I am the only one who retains my first name Lubo.

Though I am happy to have found my three friends, I miss my old buddies in Rome. Most of all I miss Mutika. I would love to see her. I think about her all the time. Coming home the last day of school, before the Christmas break, I find her letter on Kolega's desk. I sit down right away and respond to her

Dear Mutika!   *XII. 22.1945*

First of all I am confirming your letter, which I received with much happiness. I found it on Kolega's table when I came back

from school. I read it with double joy, because in school I received good grades, a 4 being very good, and thought how much they would make you happy; here they are:

Croatian	3
Russian	4
History	4
Geography	4
Biology	3
Mathematics	4
Drawing	4
Religion	5

> Merry Christmas
> and
> I send you many
> kisses!

This Sunday evening I am traveling to Slavonski Brod to celebrate Christmas and school holidays. How is it for you in Rome? Have they turned the central heating on in our House? How are all my friends and what kind of new games have they invented? Please send me at your first opportunity my 'Robinsons' (Comic Strips) and if you can buy more good ones, because here I don't have anything to read. How is Danček and his leg? Give him two packets of chewing gum, because I know how much he loves it. Don't be afraid that I am cold here, because I have a ski outfit and in Brod I will get a new overcoat.

Just like me, yesterday when I went to see 'The Blue Bird' I was so excited that I forgot my cap in the movies. Please tell Frank, and Danček to write to me. I think of you often and await your letter soon. Everything is fine for me here but I desire to see you.

Many hugs and kisses,
Your Lubo

I escape into fantasies about the Wild West written by a popular German writer Karl May who never left Germany. Characters like the Indian brave Winnetou, and Old Shatterhand with his rifles: Bear Killer, Silver Gun, and Henry Rifle, became our heroes we attempt to emulate. I use Otata's workshop to fashion wooden pistols, Tomahawks, and a bow and arrows. My friends and I make Indian headdresses from the leftover goose feathers. On weekends we pack our gear into paper bags and take the trolley to the last stop, the bridge over river Sava. We walk upstream on the embankment, until we reach a thick grove of reeds growing on a flat ravine. Nobody wants to be Indian, so we decide to change sides mid-game. I am Winettou first and strip my clothes down to my underwear, paint my face with red, white, and blue watercolors, and don the feather headdresses. Valent does the same to become my Indian cohort and we start chanting as we circle Likar and Kolar who keep their clothes on, guns in their waistbands, wearing some old hats we took from our parents. We spend the next several hours, hiding among the reeds and waging the battles we read about. At mid-day we switch, and continue acting out the stories. At the end of the day, we wash our dirty bodies and sweaty faces now dripping white, red, and blue paint, put on our clothes and return to the civilization of Zagreb.

Valent lives with his divorced mother on the fourth floor of the same building Mutika's sister, my other Aunt Rožika, lives. In Valent's attic, we find a collection of more than three years' worth of old newspapers his mother saved. For us they contain a treasure of daily comic strip pages. Valent and I spend the next several weeks cutting each day's strip and stapling them together into little booklets we sell to our classmates.

I am not very close to Likar, but all four of us spend a lot of time together. One day Valent tells us "I found out how babies are born."

"How?" We all ask at once.

"They come out of the behind."

"Who told you so? That is not how babies are born." I am not really sure how babies are born and neither are the others. But we try to explain somehow to Valent that they are not born through the behind.

"My mother's friend swears that this is how they are born," he insists.

We all laugh and let it go.

One day we are told to bring bathing suits to school. The whole day will be devoted to PE and we are going swimming at the Mladost Olympic Team pool next to the river Sava. The whole class cavorts and splashes in the large pool. I am having a great time, until the coach blows his whistle and points at me.

"Why is he picking me? What did I do wrong?" I wonder.

"You seem to be a good swimmer," he says. "I want you to swim ten laps, and then you can play again"

I swim as fast as I can, completing my task, eager to get back to my buddies. The coach picks Valent and me again and we both complete our laps as fast as we can to get back to play. At the end of the day about a dozen of my classmates are singled out and told that we can come to the pool whenever we feel like it. I am overjoyed.

Since we have school only in the mornings I spend most of the afternoons swimming at the pool. The coach makes me swim even more laps, increasing the number each time. He gives me a wooden board to swim with, and shows me how to practice my leg kicks. By the end of the summer, with these constant encouraging comments from my coach, my swimming style improves. He starts to time me, urging me to improve my speed. I am becoming a champion swimmer.

Some days, several of us sneak out with a water polo ball and walk several miles up the river. We jump in and float downstream, tossing the ball to each other.

That first summer, my swimming distracts me and I hardly think of Mutika. Kolega is busy at his job, and works late. Some days he comes home after I am asleep. Then after a while he doesn't come home for several days. I find out that he is staying at the house of his beautiful blond lady friend, Mija.

One day while reading a book I overhear the front door bell. Aunt Beba opens the door and greets a messenger.

"I have the court documents for the final divorce order; you need to sign that you received them," he announces.

"Oh, come in."

Aunt Beba is very happy and invites the man in. Her voice, much higher than usual, seems cheerful.

"Have a glass of Rakija, while I sign the receipt."

Who is getting a divorce? Why is Aunt Beba so happy? This is my first thought. My second is different. *Oh no! Kolega is divorcing Mutika and marrying Mija. Aunt Beba talked him into it. It is all her fault.*

I sulk and stop talking to Aunt Beba. I frown at her whenever I pass her or when she asks me something.

I decide to talk to Kolega and also write a letter to Mutika to ask her to try and talk Kolega out of divorcing her.

Dear Mutika!

I know very well that Kolega is divorcing you. You cannot imagine how much pain this gave me. Kolega thinks that you love Frank, but he does not even imagine that you can have a good friend. I will attempt to tell Kolega that no one in this world can be a substitute for a birth mother. I think that Beba is the one who talked him into it, because I cannot believe that Kolega would ever think of it on his own.

I will attempt to explain it to Kolega, and hope that you will try as well explaining it to him.

Kolega thought that I am not capable of discovering this, but I did anyway. And now, in my thoughts and in this letter I kiss and love you,

Your Lubo

That evening, when Beba goes to the kitchen to make dinner, I ask Kolega:

"Why are you divorcing Mutika?"

"What makes you think I am divorcing Mutika?"

"Well, I heard the man who brought the divorce papers. Beba was really happy when he gave her the papers. Why did you let her talk you into divorcing Mutika?"

"No, no. You have got it all wrong. Aunt Beba did not have anything to do with it. I am not the one who asked for the divorce, it was Mutika who asked for it so she can marry Frank."

"But Kolega, they are just friends. Mutika can have friends."

"They are not just friends. They are in love and Mutika wants to marry Frank and go to America.

My eyes fill with tears. "I want to go with Mutika."

"It is best you stay with me here." Kolega tries to console me:

"Don't you like it here with your aunts? Your school? Your friends?"

"I do, but I want you to be together with Mutika. It is all my fault." I start crying.

"No, no. It is not your fault. Sometime adults can't get together and fall in love with others. They have to separate."

I realize my arguments are not going to change a thing. I give up. It is always the same. I always have to leave, or others are leaving me. What can I do?

Resigned to the fact that I will not be joining Mutika in Rome and must stay in Zagreb I put all of my energies into my studies.

My friends and I go to the movies often. We avoid the empty theaters that show post-war Russian Communist propaganda movies in which state heroes at the end of the movie always ride on top of trains, tanks, or horse drawn carriages with a waving Russian flag on top. The stories are trite: Peasant boy leaves wife and child behind, enlists in the army, performs heroic acts, kills dozens of Germans, gets wounded, is decorated, and returns home, as the Internationale or the Russian National Anthem plays at increasing volume in the background. We are relieved as 'THE END' flashes over a huge hammer and sickle on the screen.

Like gems among the trash, imported movies from western countries occasionally play to full houses in selected cinemas. We stand in long lines to see *The Great Dictator*, *The Blue Bird of Happiness*, *Great Expectations*, and rarely, a real Hollywood Western.

In *The Bluebird* two peasant children follow a magical quest for the fabulous Blue Bird of Happiness and on their journey encounter their deceased grandparents who are kept alive as long as someone in the living world remembers them. I will never stop thinking of my Mutika.

The speech that Charlie Chaplin gives, playing the poor Jewish barber in *The Great Dictator*, brings tears to my eyes.

The film *Great Expectations*, in which a mysterious benefactor offers to transform Pip, a poor boy, into a gentleman, one with 'great expectations', had the strongest impact on me. I *am* Pip and imagine some benefactor arranging my trip to America to go to school and be with Mutika.

Of course no benefactor shows up and I continue with my schooling in Zagreb.

We share our classroom with the girls. We use the classroom in the morning and the girls come in the afternoon. We leave notes for them in the desks, but rarely get any responses. My favorite class is Mathematics taught by Ms. Sić. We study Arithmetic where, as in murder mysteries, we are always looking for "Mr. X".

Mr. Mihail Spasov, a big man with a deep commanding voice teaches Russian. We are all afraid of him. He is a former White Russian Cavalry officer, who escaped the Communist Revolution that finally caught up with him in Zagreb.

When we misbehave, he points his huge finger at the class and booms in his bass voice, "Quiet in the galleria!"

Religion classes are quickly replaced with Communist doctrine classes conducted in the presence of a teacher and run by our appointed class president Petar, whom we call by his diminutive name, Petko. He is a small stern-faced boy, the son of a local Communist functionary. He is our supposed leader. We tolerate him, avoid him, and generally leave him alone as we grudgingly listen when he reads the Communist propaganda pamphlets given to him by his superiors. Behind his back we make jokes about him.

Our Geography teacher, Mr.Tućan comes

many times to class drunk. He sits at his desk on the podium in front of the class, head propped on his hand, and elbow on the desk. He calls Likar to the map hung over the blackboard and commands him: "Tell me all about the geography of Yugoslavia."

Likar picks up the long pointer and in a droning voice begins: "The Socialist Federal Republic of Yugoslavia is a federation of Bosnia and Herzegovina, Croatia, Macedonia, Montenegro, Serbia, Slovenia, and the autonomous provinces of Vojvodina, and Kosovo and Metohia."

Likar continues to describe the borders, neighboring countries, mountains, and rivers, as Mr.Tućan eyes slowly close. The rest of the class is quiet and Likar gradually lowers his voice until you can barely hear him whisper. All of us quietly get up; pick up the football from the closet, and tiptoe out of the classroom to the playground, leaving Mr.Tućan to be awakened by the loud recess bell in the empty classroom.

We do not have a regular class in Chemistry so Valent and I join the chemistry club that meets weekly in the basement of the school. I love the magic of the experiments where simple clear liquids and substances change colors or produce gases you can light to blue, red, or yellow flames, each one indicating the final substance. I like being in control and having predictable results. I build my own chemistry lab in a small wooden crate I keep in Otata's workshop, place a small pane of glass on the bottom, and line the flasks with various chemicals. I collect empty jars and fill them with yellow Sulfur –

'S', bought in the local hardware store, iron filings from Otata's workshop, salt from the kitchen, which I label 'NaCl', and blue copper sulfate labeled 'CuSO$_4$'. Several bottles with glass stoppers contain unpleasant smelling Ammonia – 'NH$_3$' and corrosive Sulfuric Acid – 'SO$_4$'. Kolega buys me a small stand with test tubes that I place in the middle of my lab crate. Valent and I scour the local pharmacies for chemicals we can use in our experiments.

While I am busy with the numerous activities, Kolega spends more time at work and with his new wife Mija. They were married in a civil ceremony without telling me or anyone else. Mija is a pretty lady with beautiful blond hair, which she lets swing over her left shoulder. She always smells of a sweet lilac perfume. I am glad that the first time I meet her she just shook my hand, and did not embrace me or kiss me like my Mutika would. I cannot make up my mind if my Mutika or Mija is prettier.

Almost every afternoon I sit with my family in a cozy room heated by a tall green clay-tiled coal stove. Clouds of smoke float above my three cigarette smoking aunts: Beba, Rožika, and Babuš. They follow a ritual of drinking Turkish coffee after the noon meal. First my aunt Beba roasts the raw green coffee beans in a flat pan. It sends out a sweet, tangy, burnt aroma that still lingers in the senses of my mind.

She places the dark brown roasted beans in a tall brass grinder; decorated with etched designs. It is my chore to turn the handle on top and grind the roasted beans into a fine powdery dust. The water, boils in a copper pot with a wooden handle we call "Džezva", and Beba sweetens it with three heaping teaspoons of sugar followed by the same amount of finely ground coffee. Just as the brew begins to boil she removes it from the heat, allows the foam to settle, and then places it back to boil again. Beba repeats the process three times, before she pours the coffee into each "Findžan", a small teacup with no handles that sits on a small plate. Beba, Rožika, and Babuš cool the hot coffee by slurping it in a chorus that sounds like a bubbling brook.

I am too young to drink the strong coffee; besides, I hate the taste of the bitter brown brew. I anxiously wait for Babuš to weave her magic fortune-telling stories. Everyone overturns the finished cups onto their small dishes, twists them around three times. To make the magic work, they all touch the bottom of the upturned cup three times with the index finger as they make a silent wish. Three is a magic number and everything has to be repeated three times. After waiting for the muddy coffee drippings to settle, they turn the saucer back up. Inside the white cup, around the sides and the bottom, the brown grinds magically arrange themselves into twisting shapes and fantastic pictures. Everyone hushes as Babuš picks up Aunt Rožika's cup and points to a spot that she says looks like a rider on a galloping horse. I lean over but see only a brown smudge against the white porcelain cup.

"You must be patient." Babuš tells Rožika. "The one you love dearly is on his way and will be here soon. Look how close he is to the mountain on the left."

I see only a mound of coffee grinds on the bottom of the cup.

Babuš continues to predict everyone's fortune. She embellishes fantastic stories of marriages, births, death, money, fortunes, and lucky and unlucky events. I listen, my eyes wide open, wondering how she is able to see all of this just by looking into a muddy cup.

Kolega helps me with my homework and we spend many evenings together building toys or contraptions that interest me. In my history class at the "Second Boys Gymnasium" we study the Middle Ages. The ancient catapults that hurl huge boulders over the walls of enemy forts intrigue me. How can they create such destruction of the stone fortifications? They do not use explosives as the Germans did when their bombs destroyed Belgrade. I wonder how the catapults work. Kolega and I look at pictures in my history book.

"There are many different models of catapults," he explains. "Some use counter weights to hurl the stones, others use heavy springs. We could build one if you want to."

I nod eagerly. "You can really build a catapult for me?"

Soon we gather some old steel packing tape, some scrap wood and an old teaspoon. Kolega's steady hands cut the steel packing tapes into short strips and punch several small holes with a large nail. With little screws he fastens several of the strips to the piece of wood, and then with some wire attaches the spoon to the strips. The whole contraption starts to look like the pictures in my history book. I wonder how it will work. We stretch the spring, latch the spoon to the trigger, load the catapult with a marble, and release it. The marble propels in a huge arc and lands with a thud on the other side of the room. We did it!

One afternoon, Kolega comes home, serious look on his face. We sit in the parlor and he tells me:

"We will have to move to Subotica."

Subotica is a small provincial town next to the border with Hungary.

"Why do we have to move?" I ask. "You have a good job here."

"My job is the reason I have to move. As you know, I am in charge of our office and am responsible for the distribution of heating coal to the residents of Zagreb. We use a fleet of trucks that need a constant replacement of tires. I realized that there is a slowly worsening shortage of tires. By winter, we will not be able to have enough tires to operate the truck and meet the demand for coal. They will blame me."

I listen, but tune him out. This is just another excuse for moving to another place. I make up my mind; I am tired of moving. I am not moving with him.

"I don't care where you and Mija go. I am not moving." My tone is very angry.

"Well, you don't have to move right away. Mija and I will go first, find a place to live, and see how things work out at my new job."

I stand my ground. "I am never moving from Zagreb. You can come and visit me."

"We will talk about this some other time."

I don't care. I am not leaving my aunts, Otata, my friends, and my school. I want to stay in one place.

That summer I visit Kolega and Mija in Subotica, a small Northern Serbian town. Kolega is busy at work while Mija seems to be occupied with household chores, leaving me pretty much on my own. I explore the small town with a large park, and swim in the nearby lake Palić. Without my friends I am bored and very lonely. Swimming in the warm lake is not much fun and I keep thinking of how I enjoyed floating down the Sava river with my friends as we tossed the ball to each other. I brought some books from Zagreb and they provide the only escape. I look forward to the weekends when Kolega joins us. He always has a surprise: a visit to the countryside, lunch in some nice restaurant, or just a stroll through the town.

"I thought that next Sunday we should all go to the famous hot spa by lake Palić," he announces one weekend.

"What is a spa?" I have never heard of one before.

"Well, it's like a small indoors pool where they pump the naturally hot water from the spring. It is like taking a bath. The mineral water is supposed to cure many ailments."

I don't have any ailments but am happy to join the grownups and excited to see something new. I also wonder how it would feel to swim in hot water. Kolega takes us to the spa, and after paying the fee at a counter next to the entrance, we are led to our private spa room. The room has floor to ceiling tile walls and a marble floor. There are two alcoves with benches that face a round pool in the middle. The smell of rotten eggs mixed with the steam, rises from the water surface, permeates the air, and burns our nostrils.

A slanted ray of sunshine streams through a high small window near the ceiling and pierces the mist.

"Kolega, I didn't bring my bathing suit." I protest.

"You don't need one. To bathe in the spa, we must to take all of our clothes off." Kolega starts to take his shirt off.

Mija whispers to him. "Not, in front of the boy?"

"Oh. Don't worry. We are all a family here," he says.

I reluctantly undress making sure to only show my back to Mija. Then I slink to the pool and sit on the edge to dangle my feet in the water. Kolega is already submerged waist deep in the water. I stare at Mija, who faces the alcove with her back to us. Time comes to a standstill and everything moves in slow motion. Mija faces the alcove with her back to us. She reluctantly takes off her white blouse and skirt, neatly folds each item, and places them on the bench. Her blond hair falls on her white back as she reaches behind to unhook the straps of her bra. Unhurried, she folds the bra to join her blouse and skirt on the bench. Next she slides her silk panties down and lets them glide to the floor, lifts one long slender leg after the other to step into total nakedness. I stare. I cannot take my eyes away. I never saw a grown up woman nude.

Mija turns around and a pair of stiff nipples in her round breasts focus on my eyes. Slowly my eyes drift to her slim waist, her round belly, down to a few blond curly hairs that spout from a mound shaped like a pale split leaf, between her legs. With hardly any hair, she looks like the small naked girls I often saw on the beaches of Croatia. I feel a swelling between my legs and slide into the hot water, to hide my shame, and drown my erection. She lowers her eyes, as if her downward glance will cover her nakedness below. She looks embarrassed, as she majestically approaches the pool and gradually descends the steps into the bubbling water that little by little covers her knees, thighs, belly and finally her breasts. Relieved, but still yearning to see her nakedness, I am finally able to take my eyes off her. The naked image lingers in my mind, as the hot water gradually hides her body.

Kolega happily cavorts in the water, unaware of the battle raging inside me. My natural responses and desires battle with my fury for feeling as I do. Mija is supposed to be like my mother. I am not allowed to feel such attraction toward her. I am betraying Kolega. I never had such feelings for Mutika. What is wrong with me?

Mija responds to my father with just short monosyllables, and does not talk to me. *Can she see into my shame? Does she know what is going on in my head?*

I know that Kolega wants us to be like a family together, but he only creates a rift between all of us. I hate him. I hate Mija. I hate myself. I want to leave this place. I want to go back to Zagreb.

That evening I beg Kolega to let me return to Zagreb earlier and he reluctantly agrees.

Happy to be back with my friends, I resume our activities with vigor. I am eager to brag to my friends about seeing a naked woman in person, rather than the pictures from the magazines we occasionally share, but am too embarrassed to admit that the naked lady is my own stepmother. This is the first time I keep a secret from my friends. My friends don't know me anymore.

Summer is over, the results of the exams arrive, and I start High School again. Almost all of my friends are in my class and it seems just like the continuation of the previous three years.

The awareness that I have to Immigrate to Palestine comes to me very slowly. First signs that something is not right shows in the sad faces, the quiet whispers, muted conversations that abruptly stop whenever I come near my aunts Beba and Rožika. "Palestine, war, Arabs, danger, new country," are just some of the words that confirm my ill feelings.

The shocking fact, that I must leave my aunts, grandfather, friends, and all that I loved in my life, finally sinks in only after until Kolega arrives in Zagreb and explains why we have to leave.

"You know that I am the office manager of the Government Transportation Company in Subotica?" He starts.

"Yes." *What does that have to do with leaving Zagreb?*

"Transports of arms we trade with the Soviet Union for wheat and ore travel through. This is a very sensitive position and the government is pressuring me to join the Communist Party. I don't want to join the party. My only choice is to leave and immigrate to Palestine."

"Why do I have to leave?" We argue.

"We are a family and must stay together."

"Please, Kolega, I don't want to go. I want to stay here in Zagreb. I want to go to school. I want to stay with my friends, with Otata, Aunt Beba and Aunt Rožika."

"You will go to school and quickly find new friends there," Kolega says.

"I don't even know the language. How will I go to school? I am tired of moving."

No amount of begging can convince him to

leave me in Zagreb with my aunts and my friends. Again, I have to leave all that I love behind. The only things I can take are my feelings of abandonment. A piece of my life is torn from me again. I feel like the rug is again pulled out from under me, but I keep my feelings in. What can I do? The decision is already made. I have to leave.

Kefalos

A freighter, smoke rising from its lonely chimney, sits moored in the Rijeka dock.

We board by a long walkway stretching from the dock to the deck of this ship bound for Haifa. I read the white lettering; "Kefalos," meaning horse in Greek, painted on the bow. We are told it was used during World War II to transport German prisoners of war to the US.

We enter a wide opening and descend by a wooden staircase into the dark bowels of Kefalos, a floating Trojan horse. Four levels, each one with blocks of three tiered bunk beds, stretch out into the dimly lit interior. The stench of moist wool, old clothing, stale cigarette smoke, sweat, and dried baby milk, overwhelms me. Most of the bunks are already full of people: women, men, and children of all ages stare at us. We keep descending. Dim lamps illuminate our way. We finally find empty bunks on the third level below. Exhausted from lack of sleep and the long journey, I climb into the bunk and bury my head into a musty pillow.

I am back in prison - my only escape is into listless sleep.

I wake to the gentle bobbing of the ship, which left the dock while I was asleep, and is now steaming toward our remote destination. I don't feel well. My head hurts. A sour taste in my mouth, and a pressure in my belly forces my last meal out. I am seasick. I am homesick.

I run up the three levels of stairs to the deck above and clutch the railing; my cry of rage and anger followed by a gush of bile into the sea below. I break into a cold sweat. The cool wet towel, Kolega holds to my forehead soothes my headache, but not my anger and resentment for having to leave my friends in Zagreb.

After almost every meal I double over the railing spilling my insides into the sea. I avoid the accumulated urine and excrement smell of the row of wooden outhouses perched over the ocean on each side of the ship; port side for men, starboard for women.

Toward the bow of the ship, on each side, are long waist-high metal troughs with water continuously flowing from the faucets attached to a pipe above. There are a few rectangular mirrors hanging on hooks above the faucets. Several men in black kaftans, a curl of hair in front of each ear and a small round cap on their heads, stand in front each mirror. They mix a white powder with the water and stir the mixture to a smooth paste. They use the same Popsicle sticks to apply the white paste to their faces. Instead of a sharp razor, like Kolega uses, they scrape their beard with the same sticks.

I ask one of the friendly looking men, "How can you shave with just a stick?"

He smiles. "The *Torah* forbids us to bring steel to our faces. We use a depilatory to soften our beard and then scrape it off with just a wooden stick."

I wonder what is a *"Torah"*, but am too

embarrassed to ask.

I decide to brush my teeth and clean the bad taste in my mouth and approach one of the faucets. I gulp a handful of the water and immediately gag. It is salt water, pumped continuously from the sea.

Every morning, when I come up from the dark bowels of the ship, I see the same men in black caftans with large white scarves with a blue stripe across each end, draped over their heads and shoulders. A leather strap wrapped around their head holds small black boxes on their foreheads. A similar leather strap, wrapped around their left hand also holds a similar black box. They read from small black bound books and rhythmically sway from the waist up. Their lips barely move as they murmur some kind of chant in a strange language.

What are they doing? I am too afraid to ask.

I lean on the railing and look at the horizon that pulls me further and further from Zagreb. I reflect again on how I came to this point.

We finally dock in Haifa in the middle of the night. The next morning, as we wait to disembark, I sit by a porthole and contemplate the strange poster on the wall directly across from me. On the top part of the poster, above a picture of a flat crate with wings sprouting on each side, and filled with round objects resembling eggs, is a sign that reads "EGGED". On the bottom are three squiggly letters "אגד". They look like "TAN" to me. I wonder what the connection between eggs and tanning might be. *Why the wings on the egg crate? What a strange land I came to? Why did I have to leave Zagreb?*

As I sit by the porthole and look at the strange sign I feel very lonely. It is not fear of the future, but the sadness of leaving the past that fills my soul.

The smell of cabbage, onions, dust, human sweat, excrement, and vomit mixed with the fresh salty ocean spray mingle in the air as reminders of the horrible weeklong ocean trip.

Finally Kefalos, like the Trojan horse within the walls of Troy, disgorges its passengers onto the land of Palestine. Eager immigrants emerge, ready to conquer the new home; and I yearn to return to my home - Zagreb.

We board the bus with the letters "EGGED" and "אג ד" emblazoned on the side.

"What does "EGGED" mean?" I ask the driver, who speaks English, a language I know.

"It is the name of our bus cooperative."

"Why do you have "TAN" underneath your name?"

He starts to laugh. "It is the same name in Hebrew letters: Aleph, Gimmel, Daleth. It means "Union". We all own a share in our company."

The bus departs on its way to the resettlement camp south of Tel Aviv. I look through the windows to the rocky desolate mountains to my left, a sight unlike any I have ever seen; and to my right, the blue sea on the right stretches miles over the horizon from my hometown. *Will I ever see my friends again?*

We arrive to the camp and are assigned a small room in the former British military base.

Three cots are aligned against the bare walls. I lay down, exhausted. Once more sleep overcomes me.

Life in the camp settles into a routine. We are issued aluminum mess kits and each day line up in the mess hall for our three meals. Most of the days we bring our food to our room and eat it in privacy. We are not used to eating in a large hall with strangers all around.

Kolega finds out that our friend Slavko lives in Jaffa, and one day we go to visit him. Clusters of stone houses cling to the hill and spill into the seaport below. A barbed wire fence stretches around the city, keeping vandals and squatters out. We approach the Jaffa gate checkpoint, manned by several young Israeli soldiers. They check our invitation from Slavko and let us through. We walk in the deserted streets, by vacant houses, shuttered stores, greeted by an occasional mongrel dog looking for some food. Most Arab residents have fled and abandoned their houses. We ring a pulley next to a large wooden door and hear another bell ring inside the building.

"Welcome to my humble abode." Slavko opens the door and greets us with a big smile on his face. His humble abode, with its stone archways and marble floor tiles, opens to a trickling mosaic fountain in front of the open window overlooking the Jaffa port. We sit on large soft cushions, eat some delicious pastry and drink coffee, while Kolega and Slavko smoke their cigarettes and catch up with the news. Slavko picks up a big fat envelope and hands it to Kolega.

"I am so glad that you contacted me because after escaping from Yugoslavia, I went to Rome where the lawyer who rented us the Fascist's apartment gave me a packet of documents belonging to you. Since I was illegally in Italy, I could not find work and rather than go into a refugee camp, I decided to immigrate to Israel."

"How did you get such a beautiful villa?" Kolega asks.

"My Arab card playing friend, begged me to stay and take care of the house. He had to escape to Gaza. You are welcome to stay here. It is a large house."

"Thanks," Kolega says, "but we will wait in the camp until they assign us our own place to stay."

We soon discover that work is available. The next day, early in the morning, Kolega and I line up on the dirt road in front of rows of trees bursting with bright orange fruit. The owner of the orchard greets us. He's wearing a blue shirt hanging over his khaki shorts, his spindly legs and feet are planted in leather strap sandals, and his head is covered by a small pointed cap – the 'Kova Tembel' (Fool's Cap) worn by most of the settlers. He gives me a pair of clippers and a big canvas bag, with a thick leather strap that we put over our shoulders. He also shows us how to loosen the bottom of the bag to drop the oranges we pick into a large wagon. We climb up tall ladders to carefully snip the orange stems close to the fruit with the clippers and put them gently into the bag.

I climb high on the ladder, to be enveloped by the green leaves, surrounded by ripe oranges and a heavenly smell of citrus. We seldom had oranges in Zagreb and here the wealth and abundance of fruit I love surrounds me. I pick a big ripe one and with the tip of the clippers peel the skin. I pull apart the thick wedges, as juice drips on my fingers and on the ground below, and fills the air with the orange fragrance. I close my eyes and bite, fully savoring the sweet nectar.

The sweetness and the orange smell remind me of the mulberry tree in Brod and the mulberry fights we had. At least oranges don't leave any purple stains.

I slowly savor the rest of the wedges, and proceed with the work I was hired to do – picking oranges. The bag fills up quickly and I carefully descend the ladder, lean over the wagon rim, open the bottom of the bag, and spill my workload into the growing pile in the cart.

After eating many more oranges I decide to drink just the orange juice. I carve out half an orange to make a cup into which I squeeze the juice of several oranges.

Late in the afternoon when we are done with our work, we line up for the owner to pay us our wages. I keep thinking that I should reimburse him for the oranges I ate and the juice I drank, but looking at the brimming wagon full of our daily pick, I decide only to thank him. That evening, lying on my cot, some of the juice, now turned into acid, comes up and burns my throat.

Israel

Rijeka – Kefalos

Israel – Orange Pickers

Sarid – Permanent Housing

Sarid – Three Musketeers
Nathan, Simon, Lubo

Sarid – Dolio

Sarid – Beka

Sarid – Our Barrack

Lou Pechi

The Kibbutz

Most of the day, I wander through the camp, unwilling to spend time in the small barrack room, unwilling to spend time with Mija, unwilling to spend time with Kolega. *Why did they bring me here?* When not picking oranges I am free to venture into the countryside around. Walking on dusty paths between orange groves and plowed fields, reminds me of the endless Cowboy and Indian games we played in the marshes of the Sava river in Zagreb. Exiled into this strange land I wonder if I will ever see my old friends again. *Will I ever see my aunts and grandfather? Will I ever go to school again?* I hate this place.

The next day Kolega, all beaming, returns to our room.

"I just found out that Lubo will be able to go to school on a Kibbutz. They are registering children for assignments."

"Will we all go to the Kibbutz?" I inquire.

"No. No. It is only for children. Mija and I will have to stay here."

"You mean, I have to go to a Kibbutz all by myself?"

"It is just temporary. As soon as they assign us permanent housing you will be able to join us."

I am not sure I really want to join them, but am happy that I will finally be able to go to school. I start to see the pattern of constantly being taken away from Kolega. Mija just wants Kolega to herself. If they wanted to get rid of me they could have left me in Zagreb. Sometimes I don't understand adults. All that I say is:

"OK. But I hope you won't have to wait too long for your permanent housing."

The next week we take a bus to Haifa and change to a local bus headed into the Israel Valley.

The bus winds along a road that hugs the slopes of the mountains. On the right I see red roofed houses nestled among green trees, surrounded by green, yellow and brown fields that stretch to the horizon. After an hour-long drive the Kibbutz appears on the right side of the road. We get off the bus and walk a short distance on a dusty road to a grey cement building surrounded by small red brick cottages on one side and large barns, corrugated structures, a silo, and a round water tank standing on four narrow supports.

A healthy, rugged-looking young lady greets us with a big smile on her face. Her bra straps poke out of a white man's tank top that barely covers her droopy breasts. A bright blue bandana is tied Gypsy style on her head. She wears long khaki pants, and on her feet the standard Israeli two strap monk's sandals.

"Welcome to Kibbutz Sarid," she announces cheerfully in Hebrew. "I am Beka."

I smile politely back, not understanding the strange guttural sounds.

"But I don't understand Hebrew. I speak: English, German, Italian, Croatian, Russian, but no Hebrew."

She finally starts talking to me Yiddish, which is similar enough to German, which I understand.

"Ich bin Lubo." I respond in German.

"Oh we will have to change that. I know. We will call you Levi."

"Levi?" I look puzzled. I don't like that name. In Croatian 'Levi' means 'Lefty'. The name keeps reminding me that I am always left or have to leave all that I love behind.

"Why can't I keep my real name?

"We will have to change it. In the Kibbutz we all have Hebrew names. Levi was the third son of Jacob and Leah, and the founder of the Israelite Tribe of Levi."

I don't care about the importance of Levi. I don't like the name. I am tired of constantly having to change my identity. Why can I be my self – Lubo?

Beka registers me in a book as Levi, writing in Hebrew – "לֵ וִ י".

She measures me with a cloth tape, checks my collar, sleeve length, waist and size of my foot. She tries several small dome-shaped pointed caps - 'Kova Tembel', similar to the one worn by the owner of the orange grove, and leaves one that fits on my head. With the stupid hat on my head I silently stand there. From a shelf behind the counter, she picks two shirts, two pairs of short pants, and a pair of sandals, a pair of rugged boots, and places them on top of two folded blankets on the counter. She takes the stack and tells me in Yiddish "Kum!" I am to follow her.

"I better leave now. I have to catch the bus back," Kolega says.

I hug him and after he leaves I pick up my small suitcase and trail Beka to a row of tents lined up under a row of trees behind the building. She dumps the blankets on one of the two military cots in the tent.

"This is only temporary," she announces "until we complete the permanent barracks on the periphery of the Kibbutz. We are expecting a group of Bulgarian kids to arrive within the next few days."

She leaves and I sit on the cot with my new name, my new attire and a stupid hat still on my head. I don't feel like the Israeli 'Kibutznik' I am supposed to be.

Over the next few days the tents begin to fill with Bulgarian fourteen-year-olds, kids exactly my age. I am happy to finally have company. There is no problem communicating with them, Bulgarian being very similar to Croatian. Each morning we awake to the clank of a large metal triangle suspended from one of the trees. Breakfast is in the large dining hall used by all the adult members of the Kibbutz. After breakfast Beka, a long list in her hands, reads the daily assignments for each one of us. I am in a group of about twenty others and we are assigned to spread rat poison in the fields. Each is given a contraption with a long tube attached to it. By squeezing the trigger, I send several red poison coated wheat grains down the tube. We are to look for the rat holes in the field and drop the poison into each hole. At first shooting grains into the holes is lot of fun, but as the day wears on the boredom of the task overtakes me and I halfheartedly move on, bypassing some of the holes. We work six hours and return to the classroom for three hours of Hebrew lessons.

Dolio, our male youth leader or 'Madrich', is our teacher. He is a tall man in his forties sporting a big belly. His deep voice, reminds me of my Russian teacher, Mr. Spasov in Zagreb. I find out that the word 'Madrich' derives from 'Derech' which means route, path, or way of life. I guess he is supposed to show us the way. The classes are temporarily held in the dining room until our permanent housing is finished. Dolio writes the Hebrew alphabet on the board and we copy the strange squiggles in our small blue notebooks. The strange Hebrew letters written backwards, from right to left have no connection to any of the languages I speak.

Besides being tired after six hours of walking in the fields. I am upset about getting behind in my studies. I hoped to continue with my high school subjects and not be thrown back to the kindergarten level of learning to read and write again.

One day Beka assigns me to work on the compost pile. All my friends hold their noses and laugh at me.

"Make sure you take a bath before you come in. And don't forget to leave all your dirty clothes outside."

I smirk at them as I leave to report to the horse barn where I meet Mr. Goldberg, the man in charge of the compost pile. I think: "What an appropriate name. In German his name means gold mountain." The barn is warm and smells of horse manure. A pungent cloud of steam rises from a puddle under one of the horses. Mr. Goldberg, a tall man with a pronounced beer belly, his baldhead covered by the ever-present dumbbell-cap, greets me. His unbuttoned blue shirt hangs loosely over his white T-shirt and khaki pants. His boots are caked with dry manure, and I keep thinking that my almost new boots will look like his by the end of the day. I help him hitch two horses to a flat cart resting on four rubber tires. The two of us sit in the front and leisurely ride to the cowsheds. The cows are penned in two rows of metal stalls, and milked by steel suckers with black rubber hoses attached to their udders. The rhythmic hum of the sucking sounds like a mechanical factory. The large outdoor pen is empty of the cows and gives us a great opportunity to collect their dung. The sun, having climbed up from the horizon, shines on us.

We unhitch the horses from the cart and hitch them to a large scooper that looks like a giant dustpan with a wide handlebar in the back.

Mr. Goldberg shows me how to work the scooper. I have to hold down the handle in the back as Mr. Goldberg leads the horses. The sharp front of the scooper scrapes the ground and picks up the compressed dung on the ground. When the horses reach the exit, I lift the handle and the scooper flips forward and, with a loud bang, spills its load into the ever-growing pile. A cloud of dried cow dung dust rises and makes me cough. I tie my handkerchief around my mouth to keep the dust and the smell away.

This goes on for the rest of the morning. Next we hitch the horses back to the cart and, shovels in hand, transfer the pile onto the cart, sit on the dry dung in front, and again at a leisurely pace drive to the waist-high black compost pile that smells like someone is cooking a mixture of cow dung, horse urine and dried straw.

Mr. Goldberg announces, "Well, I think we deserve lunch."

We climb on top of the compost pile, sit with our legs dangling over the edge, unwrap our sandwiches, and admire the wide multicolored fields in the valley below us. Mr.Goldberg takes off his shirt and I notice the blue numbers tattooed on his arm.

"Were you in a concentration camp?"

His face stiffens up.

"Yes, but I don't like to talk about it."

To change the subject I ask him," What did you do before the war?"

Mr. Goldberg's eyes brighten up; he straightens out lifting his head up.

"I was a well respected and high ranking judge of the supreme court in Berlin. Those were the good times, but I would not trade the work I am doing now for any amount of money. Working on the compost pile is a million times more rewarding than what I did in Berlin." I am shocked!

How could he like working on this shitty

pile? I would give anything to be back in Zagreb rather than in this hot, dusty, and desolate land.

The next week I am assigned to work in the electrical shop. The cool shop keeps me from sweating with my fellow "Kibutzniks" out in the fields. I love repairing broken lamps, fans, irons, and any small electrical appliances. For me working with Old Meyer, my sixty or so supervisor, is not work; it is play.   Meyer with his bald head sprouting unruly wisps of hair above his ears, black rimmed glasses on his nose reminds me of Otata. Though Otata is very precise and meticulous, Meyer is scattered and gets things done in a haphazard way. I like how Otata works and attempt to organize to no avail Meyer's workshop. Every time I return, his mess has reappeared.

Most of the time he leaves the continuity probes touching the metal plate of the bench that electrifies all the tools scattered on its metal surface. Whenever I pick a pair of pliers, or a screwdriver it sends a powerful shock through my whole body, makes me jerk, drop the tool, and yell an expletive.

My happiness is short lived when one day I am reassigned to work in the fields. I sit on the flatbed, as the tractor pulls away from the kibbutz and into the fields. Brown plowed fields are lined with rows of bright green foliage. Occasional patches of weeds, like brown squatters, raise their heads high, and appear randomly among the green rows.

The tractor stops near a pile of various tools.

Our lead proceeds to instruct us on what our task for the day is. Each one of us picks a hoe from the stack. We start at the beginning of a row and proceed to remove only the weeds, careful not to damage the carrot tops. I don't care about carrots or weeds.

I dream about electricity.

My love of electricity started early in life, when as a five-year-old I used to connect strings of wires from the dining room to the kitchen, so my mother could buzz me. This was the signal to put several cubes of sugar into the toy freight train with tracks from kitchen to the dining area and deliver sugar cubes to my mother.

I want to be an electrical engineer, not a farmer.

Why do they insist on trying to make a farmer out of me?

Our new quarters, away from the main part of the Kibbutz are finally finished. Two stained-wood barracks, prefabricated in Sweden, have a large main room where our common activities take place and two additional bedrooms on one side. Four metal beds, mattresses and pillows are lined in each corner of each bedroom. We even have sheets that are changed each month. Across one of the main buildings, separated by a flat open space of dried mud, is a corrugated metal structure, used as a bathhouse. It is divided into two sections: Boys on the right and Girls on the left. Inside each section are wooden benches on one side, sinks on the other and a separate shower area on one end. Every sink and shower faucet has only one valve - COLD. There is no hot water. We wear wooden clogs when taking showers. We open all the shower faucets, and line up naked, to form a line with hands on the shoulders of the person in front. We clonk our clogs on the cement floor, sing a children's song about a small train that can, and march under the icy downpour of the shower. We cling to each other for courage and comfort.

Randomly scattered in the woods surrounding the bathhouse are several other sleeping barracks of simple construction, a door on one side and a window on the other. Each one sleeps four. I share a barrack with two other boys, Shimon from Bolivia, and Nathan from Venezuela. We call ourselves the three Musketeers. Nathan is the tallest of the three. He is an orphan and does not have anyone in Israel. At least I have Kolega here and Mutika in America. Shimon's parents are originally from Romania, and both Nathan and Shimon speak Spanish to each other all the time. I understand what they are saying and keep piping-in in Italian. They laugh at everything I say and constantly correct me. After several months, they quit laughing at me and don't correct me any more. I am speaking Spanish.

Our group meetings, held in the common room are supposed be democratic, but are mostly announcements by our Madrichs Dolio and Beka. They suggest we call our group "Shibolim" or wheat shibboleths. Our logo, represented by the Hebrew capital letter 'Shin', has a shibboleth sprouting out of each of the three branches.

Most of our discussions are about the inequality between our group and the native Kibbutz children. They live in nice brick buildings in the center of the Kibbutz. Their houses are heated in the winter, they eat in a separate children's dining room, have steaming hot water, and work only three hours and go to school six hours a day. We yearn to be like them. We want to be part of the Kibbutz community, but we feel like step children and outcasts. I am angry about the unfairness and demand answers, but our complaints are only met by a slew of reasons that do not make sense to us. The government does not pay the Kibbutz enough and they can't afford to pay for us as well. Their children grew up in the Kibbutz, and we just don't have the experience to be treated the same. These are some of the reasons Dolio and Beka keep throwing at us. What happened to equality what happened to sharing? This is not Socialism.

Having mastered enough Hebrew I read Orwell's *Animal Farm* and cannot find any difference between it and our Kibbutz Sarid. Dolio and Beka sound just like Napoleon and Squealer justifying why the pigs live in the main house, while the rest of the animals remain in the stables. The seven commandments about equality between all in the farm story are supposed to uphold is totally overturned in the Kibbutz as well; whatever Dolio preaches does not match the reality in Sarid.

After a while almost all the Bulgarian kids leave to join their families. They are replaced by new arrivals — children from Rumania, South America, Iraqi, and Morocco. Nathan and I, not having a place to go, are the only ones left.

During my vacation I visit Kolega and Mija. It is a hot day. The Hamsin, a hot wind from the desert, pushes the heat towards the sea. After walking from the bus station a few miles away, I sit on the doorstep of their barrack. No one is home. Rows of identical boxy wooden barracks, stretch out in all directions, spread out like a giant chessboard. Interspersed between the houses are several larger corrugated metal common bathroom and shower buildings. This is the permanent housing where Kolega and Mija are finally forced to settle. The place looks like pictures of the Auschwitz concentration camp I saw in the newsreels. The only thing missing is the electrified barbed wire fence.

I spot Mija approaching in the distance. It is too hot to get up and I smile and just lift my arm to waive at her.

"Hello Mija." I greet her, but she just responds with a blank stare.

"What is bothering her?" I wonder.

She opens the door and we enter the shaded room, relieved to be out of the blazing sun. I lay down on one of the beds next to the window, while Mija busies herself at the counter with washing dishes in a small sink and putting dinner on a gas heater in a corner of the room. She hardly talks to me and any comments I make are met with grunts or no responses. I feel very uncomfortable with Mija's silence as she angrily rattles the pots. I go out to sit on the steps. It is almost five o'clock and the Hamsin loosened its grip on the earth. I see Kolega approaching. A grey powdery mist covers his face, hair, shirt, trousers, shoes, and his whole body. Kolega works for an electrician, his job is to chisel long troughs into the concrete ceilings and walls that will accommodate the electrical wiring. I hug him and kiss his cheek, ignoring the dust.

"What is the matter with Mija?" I ask him, "She is acting so strange and would hardly talk to me. Did I do something wrong?"

"No. Don't worry. She is just not happy here. She will be fine."

I am angry.

Kolega tries to make light of everything. He doesn't really care. What about me? I am not fine. I keep thinking these things, but don't say them.

We go back to the room, Kolega takes a shower in the bathhouse across the way and we finally sit down around the table in the middle of the room to have supper.

"That son of yours didn't even greet me properly when I came home." Mija suddenly announces.

"I did greet you." I protest.

"I expected you to get up, run to me, and give me a big hug."

"But it was too hot." I protest.

You are not my real Mother. Why do I have to treat you like one? I think this, but keep quiet.

Mija continues to complain about the Israelis and the Jews.

"The Israelis are so nasty, rude, and uncultured. I can't stand them. Give me back my Communists."

She and I get into a heated argument.

"You are the one who couldn't stand the Communists, and now you want to go back to them. We could have all stayed in Zagreb. You are the one who is never happy."

I storm out of the house and Kolega follows.

"I am tired of always arguing with Mija. I don't want to see her anymore." I tell Kolega. "It seems that whenever I come Mija and I end up in a big fight. It would be best if I don't come and see you anymore. You can always visit me in Sarid, or we can meet in Haifa."

The next vacation Nathan and I spend together in the Kibbutz, neither of us having a place to go.

Kolega comes to visit me one more time. We meet in Haifa and while we sit in an outdoor café, he lets me know that he will be leaving Israel.

"A former business friend of mine, Walter Kauders owns a large transport company in Northern Italy and offered me a job managing the office. This is a great opportunity for me."

"Will I leave the Kibbutz and go with you and Mija?"

"No. I think the best is for you to stay here, and if things work out, you will join us later."

I have mixed feelings. On the one hand I don't want to go with Mija and on the other I don't want to stay alone in Israel. Wouldn't it be nice if I could return to Zagreb, or better yet join Mutika in America? *Why can't I live with her and Frank?*

Next week Kolega and Mija leave for Italy. I hug him. I will miss him. But, I can't help thinking, "Here we go again. Abandoned."

I do not go to see them off. I am angry. I don't care if I see them ever again.

Lou Pechi

Israeli Air Force

Mutika's older sister, Aunt Roži, arrives in Israel with the second group from Yugoslavia. She settles in Haifa, working as a housekeeper for an elderly gentleman, Mr. Katzeneln. I visit her often since Haifa is near Sarid. Aunt Roži lost her husband Mirko and her son Stećko in the Jasenovac concentration camp. I always looked up to my cousin Stećko, a handsome twenty-one-year-old in the prime of his life. He attended the university, and was engaged to a lovely young lady.

Both Mirko and Stećko were big Croat nationalists. They always wanted to part ways with Serbian domination of Yugoslavia. The German invasion and the formation of the Independent State of Croatia (NDH) was what they dreamed of. They were among the first volunteers for the work camps to rebuild the nation.

"It is about time we did something for our country." Aunt Roži responded.
She did not suspect that the work camps were actually death camps. Neither did her husband and son.

No one is sure of how Mirko and Stećko perished, but one of the surviving camp inmates tells a story about Stećko. He was part of a group of inmates supervised by a young armed guard, who went regularly into the nearby village to bring bread to the camp. Usually, on the way back to the camp, they stopped by the guard's girlfriend's house. She took a liking to Stećko and casually mentioned to her boyfriend that he was a handsome fellow. The guard became very jealous and one day, when they were returning to the camp, he told Stećko: "See those woods at the end of the meadow. Start running. If you reach the woods you are a free man."

Stećko starts running. The guard slowly raises his rifle to his shoulder, spreads his feet, cocks his head to one side, shuts one eye, and aims at the running figure. The tip of the rifle moves from left to right as it follows the weaving target. The guard squeezes the trigger and the running figure tumbles onto the meadow. A second shot and all is quiet. Just one more prisoner is shot; the guard can say, "trying to escape."

With Kolega gone, Aunt Roži takes me under her wing. To her I am the son she lost.

"When I went to the Kibbutz I thought that I could continue with my schooling. That has not happened. I think all they are interested is to make a farmer out of me. I want to be an engineer, but that will never happen in a Kibbutz." I tell her how unhappy I still am four years after coming to Israel.

"Lubo sweetheart, I am sure we will find a solution," Aunt Roži reassures me.

And indeed, several weeks later, she suggests a plan. "I found out from some my friends, that if you enroll in the Israeli Air Force under a special program, you can be assured to go to a technical school for a year. It is not high school, but at least you will learn a trade."

"Well, in a few months I will turn 18 and be drafted anyway, so why not learn a trade. Anything will be better than shoveling manure on the Kibbutz."

Within the next month, I am accepted to the Instrument Repair Course, give my notice to the Kibbutz, and enlist in the Air Force.

After three months of boot camp I am assigned to the Air Force Technical School. The school is in a suburb of Haifa, and I am able to visit Aunt Roži almost every weekend. Our classes, held for eight hours each day, are divided into theoretical studies and practical sessions. In the theoretical classes we study physics, mathematics, electricity, magnetism, and electrical motor theory, all subjects I love and am interested in. During practical sessions we learn how to make small spare parts by cutting and filing pieces of metal until they look like the original parts. This reminds me of hours observing Otata building the lathe in Zagreb, except that now, I am the one doing all the work. I follow Otata's advice, and use the calipers to measure each part and make sure that every part is accurate before assembling the parts together.

We learn to repair various aircraft instruments. Mangled mainsprings have to be carefully straightened and curled into their original shape until they look like brand new. Each day I learn something new. Before I realize it, a whole year has passed and I am ready to be assigned to a base.

I am sent to Tel Nof, an old British army facility near Tel Aviv, that now houses a repair and refurbishment facility, a military airfield, and an elite Israeli paratrooper squadron. In our section we handle gyro gun sights. Each day, we receive several gun sights that have to be fully taken apart, cleaned in an alcohol bath, reassembled and carefully calibrated. I mount the gun sights onto a large turntable and tweak the adjustment screws until all the test results are within specifications. When properly calibrated, the gun sights automatically calculate the correct angle for a machine gun, based on the speed of the aircraft, the distance of the enemy plane, and the rate of turn to allow the pilot to score a hit. I am very proud when I get the feedback that we scored 100% on one of the test runs.

Life in Tel Nof is similar to life on the Kibbutz, except that I don't have to work in the fields, or shovel manure in the cow shed. Once a week we line up, boys on one side and girls on the other, in the large parade ground in the middle of the base for a review. The majority of the soldiers are young and hardly older than twenty years. We wear our starched uniforms and stand at attention as the flag is raised. The proceedings are conducted by a sergeant major, his orders barked from under his large vibrating mustache.

I share a room in a large barrack with Shaul. We become good friends. I use my free time to study subjects I will need to pass high school requirements. Math, Physics, Geography, and History are not that difficult, but Hebrew, which is a big part of the exam, becomes an overwhelming obstacle to me. I just don't have the background in the language and the vocabulary of the Bible, the basis of Hebrew language.

We are free on weekends, and most of the people who do not leave the base organize group activities such as excursions to the countryside, dances, and parties. For the upcoming holiday, we decide to put on a popular musical play "Countess Maritza" by a Hungarian composer Emmerich Kalman. We build a stage, paint the scenery, and rehearse daily to finally put on the play. Esther, who has a golden voice, is cast in the main role of Countess Maritza. I like Esther and would love to sing some of the duets with her, but I don't have a good singing voice. I take the role of Prince Moritz Popolescu, a comic character in the play. Our opening night plays to a full house that cheers after each song. At the end after thunderous applause they give us a standing ovation.

I spend many weekends at the large swimming pool on the base and join the base swimming team. We have a competition within the Air Force and I win several first places in freestyle swimming. I am selected to go to the all Armed Forces competition in Haifa.

The big competition is much harder, but I manage to return with several second and third place medals.

Aunt Roži's health starts to deteriorate and I spend most of my weekends traveling to Haifa to be with her. She is brave and is afraid that soon she will not be able to take care of me. She writes a letter to Mutika and begs her to arrange for me to join her in America.

November 4, 1954

Dear Pirika,

First of all I want to thank you for your letter, but most of all for the enclosed photos of you and the darling children, which are like good medicine for me. I am not well, both physically and mentally, and if Lubo didn't visit me almost every Saturday I don't know how I could bear it.

He is a ray of sunshine in my grim life. Beside me, he does not have anyone here and I feel responsible to put him on his two feet, while I still have the strength to do it. Lubo is a good and talented boy, modest, obedient, and has potential for a bright future.

Unfortunately in this country there is no opportunity for him, and only in America can he achieve what he deserves. It is my dying wish that you will find a way for him to join you in America.

Time is running out. Next year he will be turning twenty-one and now, while he is still a minor, is the time to act.

I did not listen to you, when you begged me not to allow my dear Stećko to join the work brigade and I lost him. Please listen to me this time, before we lose Lubo.

I conclude with hope that you will take my advice and grant me my request.

With all my love to: you, Frank, and the kids.

Your Roži

Lou Pechi

The Passport

Shortly after Aunt Roži writes the letter to Mutika everything starts to accelerate. Legal papers from America arrive regularly in the mail. I am discharged from the Air Force and move to a rented room in Haifa. At 5:00 AM every day I walk downtown to my part-time job of counting newspapers. *Haaretz, Jerusalem Post, Davar, Yehidot Ahronot*: Stacks of these various papers, tied with coarse brown string, are dumped from a truck onto the sidewalk. Our crew of several men and boys swoop onto the piles, each choosing a different newspaper, cutting the strings, and counting by threes to thirty copies. Then we re-tie each stack with the remnants of the string. Our lead reads from a list of customers, and tells us where to place our different stacks so that each reseller gets the correct number of newspapers he ordered.

All papers sorted, I am free to get a cup of coffee and a doughnut from the stand and spend the rest of the day going to various government offices to collect the numerous documents, legal papers, translations, and other papers the American embassy requires in order for me to join Mutika in San Diego. I go almost weekly from Haifa to Tel Aviv to spur the slow progress of the American embassy bureaucracy. I feel like Sisyphus who is compelled to roll an immense boulder up a hill all day, only to watch it tumble back down in the evening. In addition to all the red tape, I need to take a medical examination with an embassy-appointed doctor.

While waiting in the office, the nurse asks me if I would assist her by holding down a small boy bitten by a rabid dog, so they can give him a shot. I hold one of the boy's legs as the doctor slowly plunges a huge needle in the boy's groin. The little boy looks scared and I expect him to scream and cry, but I am surprised that he only emits several small grunts. I picture myself on the table and begin to feel faint, color drains from my face, and my eyes glaze over. The nurse looks at me and, to my great relief, tells me "You better go out and sit down. We can handle this by ourselves."

One of the most important documents I need is an Israeli passport, issued by the Ministry of the Interior.

The man at the office desk, a puzzled look on his face, looks at my application. "What are you doing here applying for a passport? You are not Jewish. You should be applying for a passport at the Yugoslav embassy."

"What do you mean I am not Jewish? I can't get a passport from them. We gave up our Yugoslav citizenship when we immigrated to Israel." I raise my voice.

"Well, here it states that your nationality is Croatian," the clerk says.

"Yes, that is right. I was born in Croatia, but I am Jewish. The people who registered us when we came to Israel seven years ago, must have made a mistake."

"I wish I could help you, but the only way I can issue an Israeli passport is for you to prove that you are Jewish."

"What do you want me to do?" I ask him.

I keep on thinking, "How ironic? Half of my life I had to hide my true origin and pretend that I was not Jewish. Now in Israel I have to prove that I am."

The official tells me, "You need to get a certificate from the Rabbinical Court that states you are Jewish."

I make an appointment with the court in Haifa. The building is full of people waiting for weddings, divorces, birth certificates, and me waiting for my certificate of my Jewishness.

While I wait I'm asked to hold one corner of a wedding canopy for a couple that is getting married. I oblige, but wonder if the wedding will be legal since, according to the law, I am not a Jew.

Finally my turn comes and I'm summoned to a large empty room. On one side is an elevated platform with three black robed rabbis sitting behind a large long wooden desk. They wear identical round black hats, stern looks, and long white beards. There are no chairs in the room and I feel very small as I stand looking up to the three commanding figures. I feel like the character in Kafka's *The Trial*. He, too, is given the same absurd task of having to prove to be something he already is. The Rabbi in the middle, his eyes magnified through his large horn rimmed glasses, asks me in a raspy voice: "Please state you name and the reason you are here?"

"My name is 'Ljubomir Peći' and I am trying to get an Israeli passport. My father did not understand the registrar when we came to Israel who recorded us as being Croatian. Until I prove that I am Jewish I cannot get an Israeli passport. I hope you will be able to issue a certificate that indicates that I am Jewish."

I continue. "I was jailed by the Nazis and survived the Holocaust. I have lived for seven years in Israel. I was on the Kibbutz, and served in the Israeli Air Force for three years, and I speak perfect Hebrew."

"All of this is nice, "the Rabbi interrupts me," but we need to see your mother's birth certificate. One's Jewishness is determined through the mother's lineage."

By a stroke of luck, Uncle Slavko had Mutika's birth certificate and gave it to me while we visited him in Jaffa. I hand it to the Rabbi. He carefully examines it.

"This looks OK. Do you have your birth certificate?"

"Yes."

I hand it to him, and the three rabbis huddle over the documents as they whisper to each other.

"Well everything looks pretty good, however we have one more thing to determine."

The Rabbi on the right gets down from the raised bema and joins me down on the floor.

"Would you please step into the corner of the room," he tells me. "And, drop your pants."

I do as he orders, by this time desperate get the ordeal over and prove that I'm Jewish. He fingers my penis and examines it to see if I was recently circumcised or if it is an old wound.

Satisfied, he steps back onto the podium, nodding his head in approval. I pull up my pants and return to the middle of the room to face the three Rabbis again.

"Congratulations, looks like you really are Jewish. We will issue you a document to that effect."

I am elated. I really don't care whether I'm Jewish or anything else. I just want my passport so that I can go to America.

Aunt Roži's health continues to deteriorate. Jaundice turns her skin yellow. She tries a different diet, hoping to clear her skin. I visit her every week.

One Saturday I ring Aunt Roži's apartment, but there is no answer. I wonder why she is not home and decide to check with her friend Edna next door.

"Oh I am so glad to see you," Edna says. "Poor Roži was taken to a private clinic and I tried to get hold of you for the last three days."

"How come she had to go to the hospital?"

"She was in excruciating pain. They will run tests there," Edna tells me.

I rush to see her. The clinic is not far from Aunt Roži's apartment. I climb the steps to the second floor and enter her private room. She lies in a bed next to the window, blanket up to her chin; black hair with silver streaks outlines her yellow face. She smiles at me.

"Lubo, it is so good to see you. Did you get your passport?"

"Yes, but more important; Aunt Roži, how are you feeling?"

"I will be fine. They treat me really nice here."

I tell her all about my encounter with the three Rabbis.

"This is really funny." She laughs.

I meet with her doctor. He has a stern look on his face. I suspect the news is not good.

"We ran some test, and I am sorry to tell you that Mrs. Tkalčić has advanced liver cancer. She does not have long to live. She thinks we are treating her just for jaundice, but all we can do is to give her Morphine and make her comfortable. I would advise we don't tell her that she has terminal cancer."

With every visit, her condition worsens as my progress in getting the required papers improves. Life slowly drains out of her body. Her once-round face shrivels, as the skin sags on her bones. Her voice quivers, as she asks about my progress.

"I am so happy things are going well for you. I am getting better as well." She whispers in a raspy voice.

One day I announce happily, "I was just informed by the American embassy that the request for immigration has been granted. All I have to do now is purchase the tickets."

I don't tell her that my visa is not within the American quota system and I must rush to be in the United States before my 21st birthday. I also don't tell her that originally I planned to take a steamship to America, but since I will turn twenty-one in August I have to change my plans and take the much more expensive airplane flight. All she knows is that I can join my mother in the U.S. now.

Aunt Roži beams. I can see the relief on her face. Her dying wish has come true.

The next morning she is at peace as she joins her husband Mirko and son Srećko.

In the hot Israeli climate the burial takes place as soon as possible. A dozen friends gather at the grave. The Rabbi recites the Kaddish and several people eulogize her. I remain silent. I reflect on how, with each step of my progress her existence faded as she hung on to life, until finally her wish was fulfilled. I watch her frail body, wrapped in a cloth Tallit, slip into the freshly dug grave.

The people come forward, take the spade, and toss three shovelfuls of dirt into the grave. Instead of handing the shovel to the next person they put it back on the ground. This, according to tradition, is done in order not to pass each individual's grief to the next mourner.

"Bye, dear Aunt Roži. Thanks for all you have done. I love you. I will miss you," I whisper, as I add my three shovelfuls to the mound on top of her body.

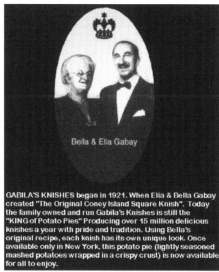

Bella & Elia Gabay

GABILA'S KNISHES began in 1921. When Elia & Bella Gabay created "The Original Coney Island Square Knish". Today the family owned and run Gabila's Knishes is still the "KING of Potato Pies" Producing over 15 million delicious knishes a year with pride and tradition. Using Bella's original recipe, each knish has its own unique look. Once available only in New York, this potato pie (lightly seasoned mashed potatoes wrapped in a crispy crust) is now available for all to enjoy.

Brooklyn – "King of the Potato Pie."

GABILA'S factory building was located in the Williamsburg section of Brooklyn since 1921. GABILA'S was a Brooklyn landmark along with Peter Lugar's Steakhouse located on the next block. GABILA'S move to new, larger quarters in Copiague (Long Island) New York in May 2006.

Brooklyn – Knish Factory

Cleveland – Kolega and me

Israel Exodus

I pack just one small piece of luggage for my trip to America. Besides personal toiletries, pajamas, and a change of underwear, I include my photo albums, my slide rule, and my notebook with hand-written mathematical formulas. Mutika wires a $100.00 money order to my stop in Rome, since I am allowed to take only $10.00 cash from Israel. Before boarding the plane I go through the Customs and Immigration. The inspector, in a grey uniform, a black officer's cap on his head, examines my passport.

"I see you are permanently leaving Israel. Why?" he asks me as he rummages through my suitcase.

"I am going to California, to my mother in San Diego."

"What is this? And what are these notes?" As he pulls the slide rule out of it's sheath and opens the notebook.

"This is just a slide rule and my mathematical formulas." My heart starts to beat faster as I worry that he will not let me leave. He frowns, shakes his head from side to side, squeezes a faint smile, and closes my suitcase.

"OK. You can go." I breathe a sigh of relief and exit the terminal to climb the boarding ramp. The stewardess points me to my seat next to a window. I am excited. Besides finally going to

America, I have never flown in an airplane.

After a long time on the runway, the plane lifts off and floats in the air. Mountains below fade and are replaced with the blue ocean below as the plane banks West to Rome.

I am lost in reverie, imagining that the pilot comes out of the cockpit and announces, "We have a malfunction in the gyrocompass. Is there anyone who knows how to fix it?"

I eagerly raise my hand, "I am a certified instrument repairman." I follow him into the cockpit, where in no time I fix the gyrocompass.

All of it is only my imagination and does not happen as I gradually drift into sleep.

A few hours later, the plane descends to the Rome airport and taxies to the terminal.

I walk down the airplane steps as I scan the crowd behind the chain link fence and search for Kolega.

I spot a small hunched man, in an oversized grey jacket hung on his slight frame, a white shirt, loosely tucked into his baggy pants, suspended by a tight belt well above his stomach. He looks like Kolega. He smiles, and I recognize his brown eyes behind a pair of black rimmed glasses.

It has been only three years since I saw him last in Israel. My, how he has changed. The strong, tall, bright, father I remember has now faded into an old man. He is only sixty years old, but the toll of the hard life ground his healthy body into the present shape. I wave back and rush across the tarmac to embrace him.

I wrap my arms around his body, my right arm over his shoulder, my left around his back. My hands clasp halfway against his bony spine. I am afraid to hug him too hard. I am so happy to see him, yet so sad to realize how much he aged. I try to repress the heaving of my chest to stop my sobs. My embrace tightens as our tears meld on our cheeks and we tremble as one.

We take a bus to the center of the town where Kolega rented a room from an older lady through the services of the Vatican charities. The room on the third floor is musty and filled with antiques. Against one wall is a canopy bed that will accommodate both of us. A large velvet curtain covers the tall windows that overlook the Roman skyline.

We sit on the two overstuffed easy chairs by the round marble table next to the window. My father and I look at each other. His eyes examine me.

What has changed?

I, suntanned, hair bleached by the sun, my body trim from daily swimming radiates health. What is going on in his mind? I wonder what he thinks of me.

My father's dense slicked down black hair, still the color I remember, contrasts with the ashen paleness of his face. His brown eyes moistened by tears glisten in the light from the window. The lips, under his hooked nose, still thick and luscious, are set in a smile of happiness and pleasure. They show the delight of seeing me, now grown into a handsome young man. I realize that he is very proud of me.

His hands shake as he opens a flimsy cigar box held together by a rubber band and some old tape and takes out several pills from one of the many bottles in the box.

"What are the pills for?" I ask him.

"I didn't want to write to you before, but I have been diagnosed with Parkinson's disease. That is what makes my hands shake."

I reach over, press my fingers around his, in an attempt to steady his hands – the same hands that built many toys for me in Zagreb.

We don't spend much time in the room and escape to the bright Roman summer sun. On the way we pass a camera store and I purchase a $20.00, 35mm Olympus camera with the part of the money Mutika sent me for the trip. We walk through familiar streets to Saint Peter's Square and are greeted by the Pope blessing the people from the high window of his Vatican apartment. I take a picture of the pope, but he appears as a small white dot surrounded by the square blackness of his apartment window. In the evening Kolega takes me to a Neapolitan Rosticeria, where we have our inexpensive dinner on wax paper as we stand against the tall counter.

The next day we depart by train to Kolega's refugee camp in Salerno, near Amalfi and Pompeii. Sadness overcomes me when I see similar barracks as the ones they left in Israel.

"How come you are again in a refugee camp?" I ask Kolega.

"Well, I didn't want to bother you in Israel, but shortly after I arrived to Italy, my friend Walter Kauders' business went bankrupt and he committed suicide. Without any work, we had to apply to the Vatican charities and they placed us in this camp for mostly Croatian refugees."

"I am confused. Who are these Croatian refugees?"

"They are mostly Croat Fascists, who escaped after the war from Communist Yugoslavia." Kolega explains.

"But they hate Jews," I say.

"We told them we are Catholic, so don't let them know you came from Israel," he whispers.

I nod my head from side to side. I can't believe that I have to lie again about my true identity. I am pulled back again into the grade school classroom, where I had to pretend to be Catholic when, during prayers, the Jewish kids lined against the wall.

That evening, after Mija prepares a nice dinner, I end up arguing with her again. "I can't stand these Croats in the camp. Give me my Communists any time."

"I don't understand. First you hated the Communists, and that is why you went to Israel. Then you couldn't stand the Jews, and now you can't stand the Croats and want to return to the Communists. This is insane." I am so angry and tell her "This argument is getting us nowhere. I am going to bed."

I am not sleepy, but I don't want to spoil my visit with Kolega.

The next day, all arguments forgotten, we visit the ruins of Pompeii. I take many photos with my new camera before I depart to America.

Then, two days later I board the big Constellation airplane in Rome and settle into a comfortable seat next to the window. I see Kolega behind the chain link fence waving to me. The propellers become a blur, the plane moves, and Kolega slowly disappears from view. The airliner picks up speed and takes flight. As it climbs, the green fields are replaced by a magnificent view of Rome.

My excitement of being on my way to America is saddened by my thoughts of Kolega.

Will I ever see him again.?

America

I sleep most of the long flight and wake to the announcement: "We are approaching New York. Please bring your seats to the upright position and fasten your seat belts."

My heart beats faster. *Am I really going to America?* I look through the window and see the New York skyline as the plane slowly descends to La Guardia airport. Yes this is it: America.

Clara Gabay, whom, my uncle Laci met years ago at the World's Fair, greets me at the gate. Next to her stands a distinguished-looking gentleman. He is Clara's father, and founder of 'Gabila's Knishes'.

"Welcome to America," he says in a deep voice as he shakes my hand and hands me his business card.

Under an image of a blue crown, the card reads, "Elia Gabay – King of the Potato Pie".

I had read many of Upton Sinclair books about the kings of industry in steel, coal, and the railroad. I cannot believe that, so soon after coming to America, I am shaking hands with an actual King of Industry.

Mr. Gabay is retired and his daughter Clara runs the business from a large table in the middle of the basement kitchen of their three-story house near the Williamsburg Bridge in Brooklyn. I sleep in the loft room on the third floor.

Early in the morning the delivery truck drivers poke their heads through the window to get the daily distribution schedules. I sit, mesmerized by my first time experience of seeing real television, as I watch the grainy cowboy movies and anything else that moves on their black and white television set in the corner. Everybody laughs at me.

Clara's daughter Dorothy, ready to be married in two weeks, is home from college. She has a lot of free time and takes me all over New York. We climb inside the Statue of Liberty and from the slits in Lady Liberty's crown I look at the New York skyline. Later Times Square overwhelms me with the hustle and bustle of its traffic. As I walk I look up at all the moving advertisements lining the skyscrapers above. I have never seen such tall buildings; they seem to be closing in on me and I get dizzy.

After a few days Clara takes me back to La Guardia and I board the plane to San Diego. After many hours of flight San Diego glistens in the afternoon sun below. The plane taxies to the terminal and I anxiously look for Mutika. I spot her standing with Frank. She is dressed in a flowery dress, high heels, and a fancy hat on her head. Frank in a brown tweed jacket, a fedora on his head, is smoking a pipe. He looks strange without his white Navy uniform. I run to Mutika and we embrace.

"Lubo, Lubo. Its' been so long. I am so happy to finally hold you in my arms." Her voice quivers, as tears roll down her face.

I am happy to see her, but I feel strange after ten years of separation.

We get in the green Dodge and Frank drives

us to their house. A six-year-old boy, head closely shaven, comes running out and jumps up to greet me.

"I am Tom," he says, and I meet my half brother.

Kathy, my eight-year-old half sister follows shyly, her eyes downcast.

Mutika says, "This is Lubo, your cousin."

I wonder why she is calling me their cousin, but keep quiet, not wanting to make a scene.

Later, when I am alone with Mutika I ask her "Why did you tell them I am their cousin, when you know I am their brother?"

"Frank's parents, Nono and Nona, are primitive fishermen from the old country. They are Catholic and I never told them that I was once married, have a son, and am Jewish. As long as I live in Frank's house I don't want to cause any problems. Please do not tell them you are my son and that you came from Israel. And pretend that you are Catholic."

My happiness to be in America is shattered. I feel like I am seven years old again, back in Brod where I had to pretend I was someone I was not. At that time being Catholic was my way to stay alive. Here it is a falsehood, which I don't accept. I am hurt.

"I don't like lying, but will do what you ask of me, only because I am grateful to you and Frank for bringing me to America." I feel like an intruder and do not want to make life difficult for Mutika.

Frank's parents are simple and devout

Catholics, completely unaware of my mother's background. Frank is the only one who knows. Mutika keeps her secrets well hidden.

Every Sunday Nona takes my eight-year-old sister Kathy and six-year-old brother Tom, raised as Catholics, to church.

"Also, you should not tell our friends you are Jewish. There is a lot of prejudice that will only work against you." Mutika continues.

Little did I know that while the McCarthy storm of the fifties had subsided, the foul smell of prejudice still lingers in the air. No one talks about it openly. The only way to detect the true odor is to be one of the insiders, one who sides, or just pretends to agree, with the ones in the know. Frank, a Navy Reserve Lieutenant, teacher, and a staunch Republican is in the know.

He never talks directly about it, but Mutika is a conduit, who not only conveys this information to me, but also adds her own concerns and advice.

Mutika is afraid to explain my relationship to my half brother and sister, without mentioning the taboo subject of divorce from my real father. She is fearful that my appearance at this tranquil setting will upset the peace. After ten years of building her "House of Cards" she cannot demolish it by telling the truth to the immediate family, acquaintances, neighbors, and close friends. The whole weight of her "House of Cards" lands on my back.

The next day after breakfast, Mutika announces, "We have to make an American out of you. Your hair is too long. I will take you to a barber to get it cut."

"OK." I say, wanting to be a real American. We walk a few blocks to a small neighborhood barbershop. There is only one chair, attended by an elderly barber. It reminds me of the barbershop in Zagreb.

Mutika tells the barber, "Please, give him a flat top." I wonder what a flat top is. I sit on the chair, the barber puts on a white apron on me, and promptly spins the chair away from the mirror on the wall. Like all barbers in Europe, he is supposed to let me see what he is doing. I ask him in my broken English "Please, turn chair, other direction."

"Can't do. The electric cord won't reach." I can barely understand him, but all I can think is "This is America."

Loud buzzing from the electric hair clippers moves close to my skin from the neck to the back of my head, like an air raid siren warning me that something is not right. I shut my eyes and am back in the jail in Brod as they shear my hair, getting me ready for the transport to the concentration camp.

I open my eyes and I see the barber slide the clippers on top of my head. Finally he spins the chair back to face the mirror. Horror! The sides of my skull are bald, while the few hairs on the top of my hair are cut flat, as if I had a runway for flies on my head.

Does this make me American? Not only do I have to pretend I am not who I am, I have to look like someone I am not.

During the next few days I develop the pictures taken with my new camera during my stopover in Rome.

The Trevi fountain photo shows Neptune standing in a shell shaped chariot, pulled by two sea horses, one calm and obedient, the other restive as it rears on its hind legs. I tell Mutika, "I threw a coin into the water. Maybe someday I will return to Rome."

The other pictures show Kolega standing on the bridge leading to Castel Sant'Angelo, and Kolega and me on the roof of St. Peter's with the large cupola behind us. I notice Mutika's mood change as I continue to show her the rest of the pictures. She does not seem pleased.

"Where did you get the camera?" she inquires.

"I bought it in Rome with part of the money you sent me."

"You mean you used Frank's hard-earned money to buy a camera? Was that really necessary? Do you realize that Frank works very hard at two jobs to make that money, and you spent it on frivolities and to entertain your dad?" Now she is angry.

I think to myself that her anger is not just about money, but rather that she is jealous of the time I spent with Kolega. She may also think that for the love of Frank she sacrificed her good life in Rome to become poor in San Diego.

"Buying the camera was not frivolous. I wanted to have a memory of Kolega. Who knows how long it will be before I see him again. As soon as I get a job, I will repay you the hundred dollars."

In fact I paid more than a thousand dollars for the airline tickets to America. Mutika and Frank's hundred dollars was supposed to be a gift to me, which I, as an adult, could spend it as I see fit. Now I am really angry.

Lou Pechi

Israel – Lubo

Fort Worth– Lubo & Judy

Fort Worth – Lubo & 1948 Pontiac

Lou Pechi

US Air Force

I have to get out of the house, and start to look for a job. With no car I take the city buses and apply at Convair, a large Aerospace company in downtown San Diego. I enter the employment office behind a door on the left side of the large lobby and fill out the lengthy application that asks me about all the details of my life. When that is done I am ushered into a glass cubicle by a lady with a bouffant hairdo and black rimmed harlequin glasses dangling on a silver chain on her well-endowed bosom. She points for me to sit on a chair next to a large desk as she sits on a swivel high backed chair behind it. She starts to look over my application.

"I see you went to a technical school in Israel. Here at Convair we really need such technical skills, but the position requires that you have a high school diploma. Since you are not a citizen and were born in a Communist country, the security clearance investigation will take too long. I am really sorry, but we cannot hire you." The lady dismisses me with a syrupy smile on her face.

I keep thinking: "She forgot one more thing. She never mentioned the real reason; my being Jewish, as well."

I get the same response from Solar a turbine manufacturer across from the airport.

I fill out the inevitable long application and am interviewed, this time by an elderly gentleman wearing a white shirt and a black narrow tie. They can use my skills as well, and while there is no requirement for a security clearance, a High School diploma is mandatory. I return home crestfallen and dejected. The biggest obstacle is my lack of a high school diploma.

After dinner I sit in the living room with Frank, who lights his after dinner cigar, while I tell him about my fruitless job search.

"Today I went to Convair, Solar, and several other companies, but they all required that I have a high school diploma."

Frank, seeing my dilemma, offers to send me to high school.

"I teach at San Diego High, and could enroll you in the senior class. You are welcome to live here, and in less than a year could obtain your diploma," he tells me.

"I really appreciate it. It is very generous of you, but I am too old to go to a regular high school with seventeen-year-old kids. I am over twenty-one. I think that the best thing for me is to enlist in the Air Force. I found out that in the Air Force, in three years, I can get my Citizenship, take a GED High School Equivalency test, take some college courses, and maybe even get a security clearance."

Frank, being a Navy man suggests, "You could also enlist in the Navy."

"I thought about this as well, but I get extremely seasick." We both laugh. I like Frank; he understands me.

The next day I go downtown to enlist in the Air Force. At the recruiting office I hand my application to a pleasant looking lady sitting behind the counter. She looks through the application, stops reading, and lifts her eyes to look at me.

"I see that you lived in Haifa. Did you visit the Baha'i Temple with the golden dome?"

"Yes. I actually lived a few blocks from it. Why?" I am puzzled.

"I am of the Baha'i faith, and the temple is one of our most holy places. Would it be OK if one evening you join our small group for dinner and tell us all about the temple?"

She tells me her name is Rina. I am surprised that she feels so free to talk about her religion.

"I would love to. I also have some photos that I can share with you."

A few days later, Rina and her husband, pick me up at the house and drive me to their friends' home. Several people are already there, and as one who walked through the Baha'i Shrine and Gardens I am welcomed as a celebrity. After a tasty dinner filled with lively conversation we gather in the living room. They pass the few small black and white photos of the Baha'i Temple to each other, as if they were expensive jewels.

I am sad when the evening comes to an end and don't want to leave the warmth and freedom of my newfound friendship, to return to Mutika's self-made house of cards. Yet afraid of upsetting Mutika's world, I continue denying my true identity even as I go through basic training at the Parks Air Force Recruit Camp near Vallejo, California.

Basic training consists of perpetual shoe

shining, parade ground marching, and barracks inspections. I am one of the older ones and the only foreign born in our squadron of young recruits. They are not well educated, having dropped out of high school to enlist in the Air Force. They want to know where I am from, my history, and background. As I tell them my story I make sure, as Mutika warned me, not to reveal that I am Jewish. I am appalled that they are not aware of the war history, the Holocaust, or the places where it all happened.

"Well, how did you get to Israel if you are Catholic?" They ask me.

"Oh, we falsified the documents in order to get out of Communist Yugoslavia" I lie.

"How did your mother remarry if your father was still alive?"

I didn't even know that divorce is not allowed in the Catholic Church.

"The first marriage was annulled," is my quick answer. I sense they do not believe me.

The tangle of my lies gets complicated and harder to explain. I soon realize that the truth mixed with lies is not believable and comes across as fabrication, and decide to stop talking about myself.

After graduating from basic training, I am assigned as an Instrument Repairman to Carswell, a SAC base in Fort Worth, Texas. The base is located on a flat plane and a large lake. On the runway, several big B25 bombers are lined up, ready for takeoff. One plane, loaded with atomic bombs, is in the air round the clock. With my lack of citizenship and no security clearance, I am kept from working on the airplanes by a double barbed wire fence patrolled by Air Force Police with their guard dogs. Since I can't work on the planes, I am assigned to the special services group, awaiting my security clearance arrival.

Initially I have a boring job of cleaning and painting the barracks, but after finding out that there is a need for lifeguards on the large enlisted men pool and the smaller officers' pool I volunteer for the job. Being one of the strongest swimmers, I am assigned to the officers' pool next to the officers' club.

First thing each day, I have a large breakfast behind a counter in the club coffee shop. A heavyset cook, with a large cook's hat on his head, takes my order, cracks several eggs into a flat pan, and with a flourish flips them over when they are done. I eat my eggs, bacon, potatoes, toast, and drink a cup of coffee before starting my lifeguard shift. I don a diving mask and proceed to skim the bottom of the pool looking for coins tossed into the pool the night before by the partying officers, their wives, and girlfriends. I divide the money with Len, the other lifeguard.

After sweeping the pool bottom and arranging the deck chairs the mornings are quiet with little activity. The pool eventually fills up with teenage boys and girls, sons and daughters of the officers on the base. Twelve and thirteen-year-old girls who look much older congregate around my lifeguard stand and vie for my attention. I am flattered, but would prefer them to be my age.

After a while I become friends with Steve and his younger sister Neva. We have a lot in common, since they lived in Italy when their father, a squadron commander in the Air Force, was stationed there. On weekends, Steve borrows his father's car and the three of us go on picnics or to movies together. Sunday is my day off, and I become a regular family dinner guest at their parent's house.

"Before dinner, my family goes to church. You being Catholic, is it OK if you attend the Lutheran services?" Steve asks me.

"No problem." I respond, thinking to myself, "Little do you know that I am really Jewish."

The base is far from the city and without a car I find it difficult to get around. I have to depend on friends or take buses that do not run on a convenient schedule. I decide to buy a car, but before that, first must learn to drive. I ask several of my friends to teach me, but no one is willing. They are afraid I might damage their cars, so my solution is to buy a car before I learn how to drive. I ask Len to come with me to a used car dealer in town so that when I make the purchase, he can drive it back to the base.

On the main street of Forth Worth, not far from the base, shiny used cars are lined in front of a small shack. A heavyset salesman, a ten-gallon cowboy hat shading his head, a half smoked cigar stuck on his fat lower lip, swaggers slyly towards us.

"Y'all looking for a vehicle? Y'all come to the right place!"

"Yes. I am looking for a car with an automatic transmission." I think that learning to drive with an automatic transmission would be easier, rather than having to worry about the clutch in a standard one.

"Well, I have this '48 Pontiac owned by an old lady who only drove it to church only once week." He winks and points to a large, four door yellow car, with chrome bumpers that glisten in the sun. It sits on four bright white wall tires. Yes, this is the car I want, but can I afford it?

"I am afraid this car might be a bit too expensive for me." I protest.

"No problem." The salesman responds. "Y'all don't have to pay me the whole amount now. You can spread the payments over the year."

I quickly calculate the monthly payment and after signing all the papers, Len and I drive the car off the lot. On the way to the base we pass the DMV office and I decide to take the written test that would allow me to drive the car with a licensed driver next to me. I pass the written test without any problems, and since I am already here feel I might as well take the driving test. Having never driven a car in my life, I fail the driving test, and reschedule it for two weeks. Later Len drives the car back to the base.

Now that I am the owner of a new car,

everyone is eager to teach me how to drive. During the next two weeks I have many instructors.

With Len in tow, I try the test again. This time, with two weeks of experience under my belt I almost pass the test. Cutting a corner on a left turn trips me and the examiner fails me.

"You drove very nicely, but cutting a corner is a violation of the driving code and I must fail you. Better luck in two weeks."

I return, determined to pass. I drive very slowly, making sure not to violate any driving codes and finally pass the test. Now instead of Len sitting next to me I can take a date to a drive in movie.

Judy

Having a car and extra money in my pocket from lifeguarding and teaching officers' children to swim means I can finally ask girls for dates. I take them to restaurants, movies or plays. To me Texas girls are very seductive. Their slow, sexy, southern drawl and intonation makes me think that they want to get romantic right away. When they say, "How *Aaare* you?" I hear, "You want to go to bed?"

When I embrace them and kiss them they don't object, but when I touch their breasts and legs they pull away. My attempts to date those girls again are rejected.

Judy, who I met at the officers' pool, is different from most of the Texas girls. She lives on a farm in Arkansas and is visiting her uncle on the base during her summer vacation. She is three years younger than me and just graduated from high school. I like her, because she is different than other girls. Even though we have different backgrounds, we have a lot in common. Judy wants to leave the farm life. She wants to be an artist, has the same interests in books, movies, and plays as I do. I also want to get my high school diploma and continue my education in college and become an Engineer.

Judy is delighted when I get tickets for 'No Time for Sergeants.' I wear a white jacket, black tie, black slacks and a dark blue embroidered tie. Judy, a bit taller than me, wears white flat shoes and a white sleeveless dress with a pearl necklace around her slim throat. After the show we park the car on the inspiration point overlooking the large lake, discuss the movie, kiss and pet. I am disappointed. I would like to have sex, but am afraid to start any advances that would offend Judy. I am afraid she would reject me, like the other Texas girls. I like her and want to see her again. I take her home and kiss her good night at the door of her uncle's house.

Judy's summer vacation comes to an end, and she invites me to come and visit her on her father's farm. Next month, I take my week's vacation and drive to Arkansas.

Their house stands alone on the edge of a cedar forest; there is a small lake facing an expanse of brown fields. I meet Judy's mother who looks just like an older and shorter version of Judy. Judy's father wears overalls and a crumpled hat, and has a pleasant jovial, bright round face with a happy smile. He proudly displays a string of half a dozen fish he caught that afternoon at the nearby pond. Judy laughs and tells me: "That is not the only thing he caught. He sips all afternoon from a jug of Moonshine he dangles on string in the cool lake."

The next morning, I watch him go to a nearby shed and hitch two horses to a plow that will crisscross fields with rows of freshly overturned soil. It is the same as when I used to hitch the horses on the Kibbutz. I pictured America, as I have seen in documentaries, with rows of combines that move in unison across vast fields, and devour the yellow wheat with their wide mouths. I am surprised and disappointed that Judy's father uses an old plough and the poverty their family lives in.

That evening Judy's mother fries the several fish Judy's father caught the previous day. On Sunday Judy takes me to her church.

"Are Catholics allowed to go to a Southern Baptist church?" she asks me before we leave.

"I am not sure, but I would be happy to go with you. I don't mind." I want to please Judy.

A small wood building, with a white steeple stands on a clearing surrounded by green cedars. Families in their Sunday best—boys in white starched shirts hanging out of their dark trousers and girls in white socks and black shoes sticking out of white dresses—line up near the wide doors of the church. We join them and then take our seats on the long pews on each side of the hall. A heavy-set lady plays the organ next to the pulpit in front.

The preacher, in a white suit that matches his white hair, approaches the pulpit, raises his hands to the sky, and shouts, "Welcome, brothers and sisters, to the house of the Lord. *Halleluiah!*"

"*Halleluiah!*" The congregation shouts back, in unison.

"God talked to my heart and opened the window of heaven. Let his word enter your soul and shine on your heart."

"*Halleluiah!*" This time everyone shouts and stands up. They sing hymns I never heard before. I feel very uneasy, but I stand up as well and mouth the songs hoping no one will notice that I don't know the words.

I never saw such loud, dramatic behavior in

any church or synagogue.

We sit down and the preacher begins his sermon. The tempo accelerates, his volume swells, and a fine spray of spittle follows every word out of his foaming mouth. He shouts at the top of his voice; his words slide into each other. I do not understand what he is saying. The one thing I feel is fear, fear of being discovered as a Jew and not a Baptist or Catholic. It is the same fear I had when I escaped to Italy and hid from the Germans. I imagine that the crowd discovers my secret and surrounds me as they kick me and beat me with their fists. I sit petrified, afraid to move, and pray the service to end soon.

What seems a century later, the preacher calms down, the congregation sings calmer songs, the service is over, and everyone gathers outside. They all munch cookies and drink punch. Everyone knows Judy, and they are pleased to see her and meet me, her new boyfriend.

When the social is over, we walk back to Judy's house. I am deep in thought. *Where is our relationship headed?* We have the same interests, we like each other, but this is not enough. As much as I like Judy, I slowly realize; I am not in love with her.

Freedom

At the end of the summer, the officers' pool closes and I am reassigned to manage the advertising for Special Services. I work in a small art room, next to the library and prepare posters and advertisements for various events on the base. The work is pretty light and I have a lot of free time to study to get ready to take the GED test. Passing that test is equivalent to getting a high school diploma. I am amazed and pleasantly surprised that many of the subjects of the test are on the same levels as the material I studied seven years ago in junior high in Zagreb.

I take the test and pass with flying colors. With my high school diploma in hand, I can continue my studies in college. So I waste no time, and enroll in the nearby Texas Christian University or as everyone calls it TCU. My first freshman class is Algebra. The class is really easy, since I studied the same material years ago. Chemistry, my next class, is easy as well, since my hobby in Zagreb was Chemistry and I did many of the same experiments in my small laboratory at home. English is much harder. I don't have any problems composing the essays, but struggle with spelling and grammar. I manage to get a passing grade. I hope that at the rate I am going, in three years, before I get my discharge from the Air Force, I might get an Engineering degree.

But, this is not to be. I am summoned to my

commander's office. "We received a report from the SAC inspectors that your Security Clearance is taking too long to obtain. Since your technical skills are important to the Air Force we received orders to reassign you to a base where a security clearance is not required. You are being transferred to the McGuire base in New Jersey."

I am disappointed. I had high hopes that I would be able to finish my studies before I was discharged. Being in the military, I have to follow orders, so I start the checkout procedure. I collect my records from the various base offices. One of my last places to visit is the Provost Marshal's office.

The officer in charge, responsible for security, is my friend. I met him while I was a lifeguard at the Officers' Club that summer.

"By the way, did you ever get my security clearance?"

"Let me look in the file." He opens a large filing cabinet. "Here it is. It came in about three months ago."

I have to make a quick decision. Should I tell him that not having a clearance is the reason that I am being reassigned, or should I just keep quiet and go ahead and transfer to the other base? If I stay at Carswell, I will have to work all day on the B25 airplanes and will not be able to go to TCU. If I leave, I will miss my friends, but I am sure to make new ones.

In some way I feel eager to leave. My gut feeling tells me to be quiet, pick up my documents and start a new life.

I finish the checkout, gas up and load my car, ready to leave for New Jersey early the next morning. On my way I have to pass Texarkana and decide to stop overnight and see Judy to say goodbye. We part as friends and agree to continue our friendship with promises to write to each other.

I leave next morning as heavy rain pounds my windshield. The windshield wipers, turned on to full, force move from side to side in front of me, in a futile effort to keep the view clear. The road ahead is murky.

"Flip – Flop. Flip – Flop. Flip – Flop." They move back and forth in an endless conversation.

"Left –Right. Left –Right." They ask me what is the right way for me?

I know that after coming to America I hoped everything was going to be right for me. I was making progress. I received my coveted high school diploma. I finally got my security clearance. I started college on my way to getting an Engineering degree. In two more years, I will get my US citizenship. I am moving in the right direction.

But I am trapped in a web of lies that keeps pulling me back—constantly pulling me back to the times when my life was in danger, when I had to hide my identity and pretend that I was someone else. I relive the fear I felt when, as an eight-year-old, I crossed the border pretending to be the son of a strange woman. I don't want to pretend any more.

I think about the times when I was happy and free, the days in Zagreb, when I played in the reeds of the Sava River with my friends. I was sad to leave them and did not want to go to Israel, but there, even though I did not like it, I was free to be me.

America promised to give me the opportunity to realize my dreams for an education and a happy life. I never expected to be ensnared in Mutika's web of lies. I do not want to inhabit her "House of Cards." I have to break out.

The rain stops; I switch off the windshield wipers. The road ahead is clear.

I realize that the transfer to the new base is my opportunity to start a new life.

I will no longer hide who I am.

I will leave my past behind and begin an honest life. From now on I will be me.

No one can hold me back.

I am free.

I am Lubo.

Epilogue

I moved frequently and lost contact with many people. However, they, as well as those whose later fates are listed below, remain as vivid in memory as they were in real life.

(Kolega) Stjepan Peći

Kolega and Mija immigrated to the US in 1956 and settled in Cleveland, where Kolega worked as an elevator operator until the company moved to an industrial park without elevators. He passed away in Cleveland after suffering from Parkinson's disease and heart problems. Mija buried his ashes in the family grave in Zagreb. After she returned to the U.S., I lost contact with Mija. Years later I found out that she passed away as well.

(Mutika) Piroska Sidon/Peći/Petrich

After her husband Frank passed away, my mother continued living in the same house. She remained very active and independent until her last days. She drove around San Diego in a 1969 Camaro. She loved the Tango and the Waltz and danced with her dance partner, Bill, almost three days a week. Two special years, after my wife and I moved back to San Diego and before she passed away, will always remain engraved in my memory.

Štefko Kirhofer

I found out after the war, that Uncle Štefko was an old time idealist Communist. He and Hanzi joined the Partisans during the war. Uncle Stefko, totally disillusioned with Tito's implementation of Communism, died of a broken heart.

Babuš Kirhofer

Aunt Babuš remained in Brod and eventually moved to an old age home in Zagreb, where she passed away in her sleep.

Hanzi Kirhofer

He remained in Brod, opening a television repair shop. He married a Serbian girl, Lepojka and had two daughters. He passed away in 2011.

Greta Kirhofer/Mokrović

Greta moved to Zagreb where she married and had a daughter Mirjana, who married her professor and had a son, Vukan, from that marriage and a daughter, Leah, from her second marriage to Željko Devčić. When he turned sixteen, Vukan decided that since his mother, his grand mother, and his great grandmother were Jewish, that he was Jewish as well. He converted, became an observant Jew, and is now lecturing philosophy at the Yeshiva University in Israel.

(Apuci) Ignatz Sidon

My grandfather Apuci refused to leave Zagreb. He never hurt anyone and could not comprehend that others would hurt him. He was arrested and either gassed by truck exhaust CO pumped back into the transport trucks, or gassed in Auschwitz. His candle was extinguished before he could illuminate my life.

(Marci) Mark Sidon

My uncle Marci married an Italian girl, Enrica, whom he met while delivering food to the family hiding in her house in Rome. Enrica and Uncle Mark came to the United States as guests of President Roosevelt and settled in San Rafael, California. They had two children Terry and Joyce. Marci, Enrica and their son Terry are now deceased.

Larry Sidon

The Germans at the beginning of the war captured Larry, shortly after he first put on his Yugoslav Officer's uniform to report to his unit after the bombing of Belgrade. He spent three years in Germany as a prisoner of war. After the war he was repatriated to his native Yugoslavia. Disillusioned with the Communist regime, he escaped to Austria and eventually immigrated to the United States. He married Irma and settled in San Diego, California. He and Irma passed away several years ago.

Milan & Anika Weber
After the war Milan and Anika both returned to
Zagreb only to immigrate to Israel in 1948. They
lived in a converted wooden shipping container in
Haifa where I visited them several times. Eventually
they immigrated to Canada.

Slavko Brenner
Slavko joined the Partisans in Yugoslavia and was
arrested by them for illegal black market activities.
After his release from jail, he escaped Communist
Yugoslavia to Italy. Upon his arrival in Rome, he
was alerted by some of his gambling friends that
there was a warrant for his arrest in connection with
paintings stolen from the Fascist's apartment we
lived in Rome during the war. Uncle Slavko
immediately left for Israel and settled in Jaffa where
he married a Bulgarian lady and became the father
of a beautiful little daughter. I visited him several
times, but lost contact after leaving Israel.

Ivo Likar
Ivo immigrated to England, to study and become a
Heart Surgeon. Eventually he relocated to Canada.

Juro Valenteković

Juro remained in Zagreb and earned a Ph.D. in Chemistry. He married his graduate school classmate Malila and settled with their two sons in Palos Verdes, California after arriving from Canada. I connected with him through our daughter Nina, who lived in the same dorm as Juro's son. Juro arranged for us to meet in a Los Angeles restaurant with Ivo Likar. Meeting my childhood friends after so many years was an overwhelming emotional experience. Their features had matured and aged, but the spirit in their eyes remained the same.

Boris Kolar

Boris was the only one who remained in Zagreb. He became a famous animated film artist. He sent me a Christmas card and I attempted, but failed to see him during one of my visits to Zagreb.

Nathan Millman

Nathan was an orphan and didn't have any relatives in Israel. He remained in Kibbutz Sarid and after I left Israel, I lost contact with him.

Shmuel

Shmuel left the Kibbutz shortly after my departure we never communicated again.

David
David rejoined his parents on a Moshav, a cooperative agricultural settlement, in southern Israel. We visited several times while I was in the Israeli Air Force, but eventually lost contact with him as well.

Milica Müller
Her fate is unknown, but after the war, Mrs. Müller was tried and convicted by the Communists as a Nazi collaborator.

Clara & Dorothy Gabay
Clara continued to run the family business from the basement of their house. I visited her with my family in the 1970s. She passed away several years later. Her daughter Dorothy and her two granddaughters moved to San Diego and kept in touch with my mother. After we moved from San Diego, I lost contact with Dorothy and her daughters.

Toma
Several years ago I visited the location of Toma's barbershop. It is now a fast food fried fish restaurant.

(Freddy/Bubi)Fred Sidon

After the end of the war Fred, his mother, grandfather and uncle immigrated to Argentina. Fred subsequently came to the US, joined the Air Force and after his discharge pursued a successful career in Management Training. He and his wife Diane live in Santa Barbara and have three sons and several grandchildren.

Mirče

I often wondered but never knew whether Mirče, being Roma, survived the war. The Nazis in the Independent State of Croatia (NDH) and in all the Nazi-occupied countries, targeted the Jews as well the Roma (Gypsies) for a total annihilation.

Rožika, Beba, and (Otata) Ljudevit Peći

Otata, Rožika, and Beba hid in a small village in Bosnia and returned to their apartment in Zagreb after the war. Otata passed away at 82 after being hit by a car at an intersection. Beba passed away after a short illness. Rožika visited us in San Diego and died shortly after returning to Zagreb.

Kathy Petrich/Britt

After graduation from college, my sister Kathy married Allan Britt who was pursuing a medical degree. They both lived in Saudi Arabia, where Allan worked as a Nuclear Medicine Radiologist. After returning to the US they settled and still live in Phoenix, Arizona.

Tom Petrich
My brother Tom lives in Temecula, California. He is married and has two grown up twin boys and a daughter.

Judy
I corresponded with Judy for almost a year after we parted. She left the farm briefly to study art in Little Rock, and returned to marry a local farmer boy.

Reader Guide

1. What is this book about?
2. What are some of the major story messages?
3. What are some of the ironies in the book?
4. How does Lubo change throughout the story?
5. What is Lubo's journey?
6. How is Lubo's fear expressed?
7. What keeps Lubo going?
8. What saved Lubo's identity?
9. What is the relationship of father (Kolega) and Lubo?
10. What is the relationship of mother (Mutika) and Lubo?
11. What is the relationship of other characters and Lubo?
12. What is the allegory of the pig slaughter?
13. What is the symbolism of the nanny character?
14. What is the symbolism of the haircuts?
15. What is the symbolism of name changes?
16. Why is Lubo fascinated by the Gulliver story?
17. Why is Lubo's reaction to the last scene of the opera Aida?
18. What is Lubo's attitude towards the Nazis?
19. What are some of the similarities and differences between the German and the American soldiers?
20. How is Zagreb different after Lubo's return?
21. What does Lubo learn from his grandfather (Otata)?
    How would you as the reader respond to some of the events in the book?

Made in the USA
San Bernardino, CA
25 March 2019